Dear Paula,

   God's Blessings of
grace and peace be
ever with you.

   Warmly, in Christ

   Kennon L. Callahan

   July 27, 2000

TWELVE KEYS FOR LIVING

Twelve Keys for Living

Possibilities for a Whole, Healthy Life

Kennon L. Callahan

Jossey-Bass Publishers
San Francisco

Jossey-Bass books and products are available through most bookstores. To contact Jossey-Bass directly, call (888) 378-2537, fax to (800) 605-2665, or visit our website at www.josseybass.com.

Substantial discounts on bulk quantities of Jossey-Bass books are available to corporations, professional associations, and other organizations. For details and discount information, contact the special sales department at Jossey-Bass.

For sales outside the United States, please contact your local Simon & Schuster International Office.

 Manufactured in the United States of America on Lyons Falls Turin Book. This paper is acid-free and 100 percent totally chlorine-free.

Library of Congress Cataloging-in-Publication Data

Callahan, Kennon L.
   Twelve keys for living : possibilities for a whole, healthy life /
   Kennon L Callahan.—1st ed.
     p. cm.
   Includes index.
   ISBN 0-7879-4140-9 (alk. paper)
   1. Christian life. I. Title.
  BV4501.2 .C2453 1998
  248.4—ddc21   98-9092

FIRST EDITION

HB Printing   10 9 8 7 6 5 4 3 2 1

CONTENTS

*This work is dedicated to
our many friends and family across the planet.
Your love and encouragement,
your laughter and joy,
your passion for life,
the ways in which you have grown forward
in living whole, healthy lives—
for all these gifts with which you bless our
lives,
we are most grateful.*

Kennon L. and Julie McCoy Callahan

PREFACE

THIS BOOK SHARES twelve possibilities helpful in developing a whole, healthy life.

You will benefit from *the stories and parables* in the book. Decisive events change our lives and shape our destinies. The book includes some of the events, decisive and helpful, in my own life and in the lives of many persons with whom I have had the privilege of sharing. These events have provided some of my most helpful learnings about life. In the seminars I have led, countless people again and again have taught me that these stories and parables are among the most helpful ways they have learned about the possibilities for a whole, healthy life. They frequently ask when these stories and parables will be available in print. This book includes many of them, and you will gain insights into living as you discover them.

The *wisdom and experience* will be helpful to you. I want to thank the thousands of persons who, across the years, have shared their wisdom and experience with me. Some are rich and famous, notable leaders in their fields. Most of the persons who have talked with me are everyday, ordinary-life people. Ditch diggers and school teachers. Farmers and busboys. Nurses and railroad workers. Housewives and philosophers. Engineers and salespersons. Ministers and educators. Cooks and grocery clerks. Insurance adjusters and hearing-aid manufacturers. Chemistry teachers and computer salespersons. Flight attendants and shoe representatives. I am most grateful for our friendships.

It is remarkable how openly and honestly people share their grapplings and learnings about life. Sometimes, in these conversations, people share their experience, the words rushing, tumbling out like the course of a mountain stream moving swiftly forward with the new spring snowmelt. Sometimes, the learnings are shared in halting, painful ways, as old memories and lost hopes are relived. Some share their wisdom, catching their breath, pressing on, with almost a half gulp of new air, with a rainbow of promise in their eyes.

The *keys and possibilities for living* will help you develop your life. This book helps puzzle through the twelve keys for a strong, healthy life. Many persons have taught me what they find helpful in living life. Their spirit, enthusiasm, excellent ideas, good suggestions, and helpful questions have contributed much. We have shared informal conversations, visits over meals together, interviews, and group discussions. I have learned much. In these conversations, the twelve possibilities and insights shared in this book have been persistently present. These possibilities and insights are drawn from the lives of persons with whom I have the privilege of sharing. The conversations include persons from the United States, Korea, Canada, Australia, New Zealand, Africa, South America, the Caribbean, England, Europe, the Pacific Rim, and China.

The more I listen, the more I learn. I measure the value of the events I do as much by how much I learn during the event as by how much I share. I learn by the questions, the suggestions, and the conversations. It is extraordinary what people can teach you when they are given half a chance.

After one event, a number of us were standing around sharing, enjoying the closeness of our fellowship. It was one of those rare times in life where you know you are really family together. Sue said to me, "Dr. Callahan, thank you for how your books are helping our congregations. We are stronger for them. I especially thank you for what your writings contribute to my own life. I began to apply the principles of the Twelve Keys in my church. I found they help greatly with my own life. When are you going to write the book that directly helps us with our lives?"

Many persons have come up to me during seminars, visited with me after major convocations, written me personal letters, asking much the same question. I thank Sue and the many, many persons who have encouraged me to develop this specific book.

I have included *the prayers and scriptures* to enrich your devotional life. People again and again teach me they have found these helpful in growing their lives forward. The prayers and scriptures enrich our understanding of everyday, ordinary life. They give us resources with which to build a strong, healthy life. Read the book with a sense of joy, laughter, deep thought, prayer, and expectancy.

You will discover an easygoing, good-fun, good-times rhythm in the book. It has been a delight to let the book unfold in a spirit of close, personal prayer, in a spirit of wonder and joy, new life and hope. Have fun with the book. It draws on our mutual wisdom and experience, our hopes and traditions, our scriptures and our prayers. You will gain wisdom, new discoveries, and renewed confidence.

───────── o ─────────

I thank Greg Brandenberg for his exceptional leadership in bringing this book into being. Greg is a remarkable person. He is among the best per-

sons I know in the publishing field. It has been a real joy to share our friendship and working relationship during these past sixteen years. He has contributed much to advancing the Twelve Keys books across the planet.

I thank Jossey-Bass Publishers for the creative, constructive way they
have moved this book forward to publication. Debra Hunter, senior vice
president and publisher, has given excellent leadership. Her insight and
judgment have been invaluable. She has built an extraordinary team of
people at Jossey-Bass. They are among the very best in the field.

Sarah Polster, as senior editor, has advanced the book immeasurably.
Her depth of wisdom, her insights and creativity, her clarity and suggestions have meant much. Sarah brings a remarkable perspective and wealth
of experience to the book, and it is much the better for our having worked
and shared together on it. The mutual collaboration has been excellent.

Carol Brown, marketing manager, has been especially helpful in making
the book widely available—to the benefit of countless persons. Julie and
I look forward to working and sharing together with Jossey-Bass for many
years to come.

Julie McCoy Callahan has contributed immensely both to my life and to
the writing of this book. For her love and wisdom I am humbly grateful.

The Twelve Keys books, emerging in the past sixteen years, now cover
the world. It is amazing to me the journeys the books have taken. They
have a life of their own. Julie and I are thankful the books are helpful with
so many thousands of persons all across the planet. May this book be
especially helpful to you. May the grace and peace, the joy and hope of
God's blessings be with you.

June 1998   KENNON L. CALLAHAN

Twelve Keys for Living

I

CLAIMING GOD'S GIFTS

IT WAS THE NINTH INNING. We had "last bats." We were three runs behind. There were two outs. No one was on base. We were playing late that Saturday night for the citywide championship. We were sort of sitting in the dugout, kicking our cleats into the dirt, waiting for the inevitable end. The championship we had worked so hard for all season was slipping from our grasp. Even our people in the stands were packing up, getting ready to leave, gathering up their things to beat the rush.

Our next batter hit a single and made it to first. A little titter of excitement in the dugout. Not much in the stands—still packing. Our next batter had the good sense to stand there and do nothing. He got a walk. We now had two men on base. There was a little more excitement in the dugout. Still, it was the bottom of the ninth, two outs. Mostly, our people in the stands were still packing. A few were beginning to wonder whether to stay and see what happened.

Our next batter hit a blazing grounder to the shortstop, who bobbled the ball and before he could make the forced play at second that would win the citywide championship, our man had gotten there, so he threw to first but the throw was late. We now had the bases loaded! Two outs, bottom of the ninth, three runs behind. The citywide championship was once again within our grasp!

The excitement, the cheers, the carrying-on, the hugging, the back-slapping—more injuries occur at this point in a game than any other, and the shouting happening in the dugout were all amazing to behold. Our people in the stands had decided it was worth staying. They were on their feet, cheering to the high heavens. We now had the chance, once again, to be citywide champions.

Amidst all this hullabaloo, Bobby—the batter on deck—had gone faithfully and dutifully to the plate, to do his dead-level best for the team.

I

When my guys saw who was standing in the batter's box with the city-wide championship now resting on the line, the words they shared with their beloved coach—namely me—are words I cannot share in this good company. Bobby had successfully struck out every time he went to bat that season.

Quick background. Bobby's father had come to me at the beginning of the season. He had said to me,

> We had our son late in life. We were in our forties when he was born. He has mostly grown up among adults. We may have played catch a couple of times in the backyard. He has never owned a glove or a bat. He has never been on a team. We think it would be helpful to Bobby's development if he could just practice with your team.
>
> We wouldn't expect him to play in the game. We know the record your team has had in previous seasons. Maybe during the game, he could serve as batboy, or something. We would deeply appreciate it if he could simply practice with your team. We think it would help him.

I said to Bobby's father, "I have a problem. My philosophy, my policy, is whoever comes to practice plays. What you can count on and depend on is when Bobby comes to practice, he will play. I'll try to see that he doesn't get into a spot where he is over his head."

Those last words were turning out to be prophetic, fateful words; he was clearly over his head late that Saturday night.

Bobby, you see, was a sucker for high, outside pitches. Everybody in the league knew it. Their best pitcher knew it, and you could see the gleam in his eye. Bobby had done nothing all season. Bobby would do nothing tonight. The championship was now theirs for the taking.

Sometimes, coaches make interesting decisions. I thought about our season as a team. I looked to the stands and saw two parents, fearful, anxious, worried, not certain they really wanted their son to be standing at that point in the galaxies he was currently occupying.

I said to the team, "We've come through the season together as a team. We will finish the season as a team. Bobby stays." The words that greeted that announcement are words I cannot share in this good company either. I learned new words I had not heard before. The team's loud complaining dwindled to a lesser mumbling and finally ground to a depressed silence. They knew the championship was lost.

First pitch: high, outside, wild swing, strike one. You could hear the groans in the dugout.

Second pitch: high, outside, wild swing, strike two. You could see our people in the stands again packing up.

Third pitch: high, outside, no swing. Bobby was tired from the first two swings. The bat stayed on his shoulder. Ball one.

Fourth pitch: high, outside, wild swing.

The best way to describe what happened is, the ball hit the bat! With just enough force that, in a peculiar kind of blooper way, it sailed just high enough over the first baseman's outstretched glove so that he couldn't reach it. It hit fair, and with a crazy kind of spin, bounced foul.

Night game, lights on, still there are shadows. The first baseman turns, hunting and searching for the ball, knowing the game is at hand.

My guys are running! I had had the hit-and-run on for every one of those high, outside, wild pitches. They had big leads off the bases. They were moving. The man from third was virtually home. The man from second was headed to third. The man from first was almost to second. Everyone was running, except for one person, Bobby, who was still standing at home plate.

My guys encouraged Bobby, helped him know where he needed to be next. With a kind of dazed expression on his face, Bobby headed for a new stage in life—namely, first base. He had never been there before. As Bobby was moving to first, the man from third made it home. One run scored. The man from second rounded third, heading home.

The pitcher had made the fatal mistake. Bobby had done nothing all season. He thought Bobby would do nothing tonight. So the pitcher had stayed on the mound, waiting to receive the accolades of the crowd for winning the championship. Normally, he would have moved to cover first base, but now there was no one covering first base.

By the time the first baseman found the ball, Bobby was near enough first base that the baseman saw Bobby would make it, so he did the next best thing he knew how to do. The man from second had rounded third headed toward home. The first baseman threw home to force that out. With the confusion of the moment, he hurried his throw, threw high, and the ball went into the cage. Our second run scored.

While the catcher was chasing the ball, Bobby rounded first, heading toward second. The only way the catcher could see to win the game now was to try to throw out the man who had come from first and was heading into third in a diving slide. The catcher threw the ball, and for whatever reason, he threw it through the third baseman's legs, out into left field.

We've all seen this before. When things start going wrong, they begin to collapse all over the field. Mostly, it had happened with my teams. I could empathize with the other team's coach that night. By the time the left fielder got the ball, the player who had slid into third had picked himself up and made it home. Three runs had scored.

The only player still running the bases was Bobby, who was headed to second.

The left fielder threw the ball to the second baseman to cut Bobby off as he was arriving. Again, for whatever reason, the ball went high over the baseman's glove and headed back out into right field. Bobby rounded second, getting up a head of steam.

One of the things Bobby knew how to do best was run. Meek, quiet, shy Bobby. He had learned to run mostly through first and second and third and fourth and fifth and sixth grades and beyond, because the teasers, the bullies in each class would pursue him, jeer him, taunt him, try to beat him up. So over the years, even as he was bashful and timid, the one thing Bobby had learned to do was run—mostly away from people who were chasing him.

Now, Bobby was running for the team—it was a new experience for him! With a full head of steam, he rounded third base, heading for home!

The first baseman found the ball. He now had his second chance to save the game, the season, the championship. He remembered what he had done the last time. You could see it in his eyes. He had hurried the throw. This time he would take his time. The last time he had thrown high. This time he would throw low. Sure enough, the ball was slow and low. It bounced in the dirt. Just as it was bouncing into the catcher's outstretched glove, Bobby lunged with all his being, so that his hand would touch the plate before the catcher could get the ball. He gathered up everything he had so he could do his overwhelming best for the team.

His hand reached the plate before the catcher had the ball! We were four runs to three! Citywide champions!

My guys did the right thing. They picked Bobby up, put him on their shoulders, and carried him all around the field. He was the hero of the season. I saw two parents sitting in the stands, tears gently streaming down their cheeks. Their son had come of age.

To be sure, late that Saturday night, in a remarkable, memorable kind of way, we became citywide champions. Even more important, Bobby came of age.

He used the one strength, the one competency with which he was blessed. He used the one talent and resource he had. He used his ability to run—with all his being and with all his might—to do his best for the team. Whether we had won the citywide championship or not, the remarkable miracle of that night was that it was a new Bobby lunging for the plate, his hand outstretched, doing his best for the team.

You could almost see it in him, as he made the pilgrimage toward first, rounded second, headed toward third. You could see a growing confidence in his stride, an increasing strength in his step. You could see him as he headed from third toward home, gathering up all of his energy, resources, being. He intended to do everything he could for the team that had seen him through the season of his life.

I have this confidence: God makes all things new. Something as simple as a citywide championship becomes the occasion in which Bobby becomes a new person. The miracle of that night was the new Bobby in the lunge to the plate. In the time, come and gone, since that extraordinary evening, he has grown in his competencies, in his relation with God, and in his strong sense of mission. And the contributions Bobby has made in his community and across this country are amazing to behold. It began that night.

It is amazing how God works through simple events to help people discover their best, true selves. Bobby claimed well the strength he had: running. He used it remarkably to build for himself a new life. Rather than running away, timid, bashful, shy, this was the new Bobby who ran toward that catcher—the formidable, massive, huge, all-star catcher of the season. It was the new Bobby who lunged with all his being to do his best for the team. Even in simple events, God helps us discover our best, true selves. We become new persons.

Claim Your Strengths

I claim my strengths. Write these words in your calendar. Put them on your mirror, at your workbench, in your car, at your desk, in your kitchen, at your sewing machine. Where you will see them frequently. Say them each morning as you arise. Each night as you go to sleep. Make these words ever present in your life.

God invites you to claim your strengths. The art, the first step, in developing a strong, healthy life is discovering new ways to claim your strengths. We have all been Bobby in some way. In life, even when it seems like the ninth inning, two outs, three runs behind, your best way forward is to claim your strengths, however feeble and fragile they may seem to you.

Look first for your strengths, not your weaknesses. Some persons live their whole life through, hardly ever claiming their strengths. They are preoccupied with their weaknesses. Sally and Josh have spent much time over the years discussing all the mistakes they have made, and the decisions they wish they had made differently. "We should have moved to California when we had the chance. When Tom wanted us to come and help him get his new dealership up and running, we should have gone. We'd have been better off." But Josh didn't have his degree—"I had to quit school to support my mother when my father died." "And we didn't have a dependable car—Josh usually took the bus to work at the factory." Their lament is, "if only such and such had happened, we would be better off." They focus on their problems, needs, and shortcomings. Sensible persons, developing a strong, healthy life, look first for what they have going for them. They look for their lead strengths.

Look first for your strengths. At the first practice of the season, as the players show up, the wise coach looks first for what the team has going for it this season:

Is this the year of power, blocking, running?

Is this the year of speed, quickness, passing?

The wise coach matches the plays with the players, builds on the strengths that are there.

The wise choral director, first rehearsal, as the singers show up, looks first for what the choir has going for it:

Is it in the alto, tenor, soprano, or bass section?

Is it the group's sense of rhythm, spirit, and enthusiasm?

The wise choral director matches the songs with the singers, builds on the strengths that are there.

One mistake we make as we live life is to look first for our weaknesses. Sometimes, that is our old, old friend, a compulsion toward perfectionism, showing up yet another time in our lives. Sometimes, it is because some loved one, who really intended good for us, helped us learn a pattern of focusing on our weaknesses. For whatever reason, we are drawn to our weakest weaknesses.

I have this confidence: God invites you to claim the strengths God gives you. The art is to claim the competencies with which God has blessed you. This is the first step toward a whole, healthy future. Use your strengths well for the team God has placed you on, in ways that count well for you, your family and friends, your community and world.

God's Gifts

I claim God's gifts. When you claim your strengths, you claim God's gifts. Whatever strengths and competencies you have, you have because God has been and is now, this very moment, living, moving, and stirring in your life. God's compassion and spirit are extraordinarily present in your life. Your strengths are gifts from God. God invites us to claim our strengths.

The immensity of the universe teaches us the immensity of God's love for us. As we increasingly discover how vast the universe is, we discover how vast God's love and care for us are. It is not true that the bigger the universe, the more distant, the more remote God is. When you think of the largeness of the universe, know, with confidence, that God's love for you is that large as well.

Sometimes, we deny our strengths. On occasion, almost defiantly, we renounce and reject our strengths. Or, we abuse them, and yield to a low-grade tendency toward self-destruction. We are our own worst enemy. Sometimes, we ignore our strengths, living as though our strengths do not exist. Or we neglect to grow them. They wither and decay.

When we deny our strengths, we deny God's gifts, and we deny God. Some of us live half our lives through, looking down on ourselves, thinking more poorly of ourselves than we have a right to, suffering from low self-esteem. We deny the God whose love for us is deeper than all the oceans and vaster than all the universes. When we have a lower estimate of ourselves than God does of us, we think our low self-opinion of ourselves is more accurate than God's strong opinion of our worth and value. In an inverse sort of way, we place ourselves above God.

It is not that we should think more highly of ourselves than we have a right to. We all have our faults, failures, and mistakes. We have our simple sins, and we have our dark, terrible sins. But we live and love life best when we claim the strengths, gifts, and competencies with which God is blessing us. Claim your strengths. When you do, you claim God's gifts.

Only You Can

Only I can claim my strengths. Do not look to other people to claim your strengths for you, or, for that matter, to grow them for you. When you claim your strengths, you claim your growth. Other people can affirm your strengths and help you discover them. They can suggest ways you can develop your strengths. Other people are possible sources of confirmation and encouragement. Only you can discover and grow your strengths. God invites *us* to claim our strengths.

Betty was always doing everything for her son, John. She looked after his every need, and more. She always knew what was best for him. Sometimes, well-intentioned persons, who think they have your best interests at heart, try to grow you for you. Their effort at growth is usually in areas where they think you should grow, rather than in areas that match the key strengths you really have. They create, sometimes unwittingly, sometimes intentionally, a codependent-dependent pattern of relationships. They do too much for you. The result is that you have no ownership of your growth as a person. You gain no practice in the art of growing yourself.

You are the person who has grown your current strengths forward. You can grow you. No one else can grow you. God knows this. God does not try to do it for you. God gives you your initial gifts, strengths, and competencies. God serves as encourager, nurturer, coach, and mentor as you grow your strengths forward. God is with you.

Grow the Strengths You Really Have

I am growing the strengths I really have. Discover the strengths you really have, not the ones you wish you had. Sometimes, we become too preoccupied with our problems, needs, concerns, weaknesses, and shortcomings. We allow ourselves to be distracted, and overlook the solid strengths we have.

Jennifer was particularly concerned to please her mother, and her mother kept urging her to become a nurse, something her mother had always wanted to do herself. Her mother said that by being a nurse, Jennifer could always have a way to support herself. Jennifer caved in to her mother's wishes. She reluctantly pursued that course of study—all the time wishing she had the special "way with people" that many in her nursing class seemed to have. As a nurse, Jennifer never felt the confidence and assurance she wished for, but her mother's approval had been so important that she had turned away from her own strengths in mathematics. After much travail, she was finally able to give up placating her mother, earned her business degree, and found fulfillment as a certified professional accountant.

We get caught up in wishing for strengths we do not have; we miss the strengths we have. Or we focus on the ones someone else thinks we should have, ought to have, or must have. God invites us to claim our strengths.

Given our desire for approval, we sometimes allow ourselves to be drawn into focusing on what other persons think we should grow as strengths, hoping that in doing so we will gain their acceptance. It is a false hope. In the end, they are never satisfied, and neither are we. Jennifer made the effort to placate and please all those around her. She was always exhausted, and they were never pleased. They always demanded more.

The art is to grow our strengths, rather than the ones we wish we had, or those someone else thinks we should have, or even the ones someone else has. The devil has a device called envy, with which he seeks to convince us that the strengths some one else has are the strengths we should have, and the devil thereby distracts us from the strengths we really have. Envy is not a friend. With wistful, wishful envy, we wish another person's strengths were ours. The consequence is that our strengths wither, and so do we.

Claim your strengths. You will grow a strong, healthy life. God wants for you an abundant life.

All Things New

I have known people in their late eighties who live with the confidence that some of their best years are before them. They are not disappointed. I have know persons in their early thirties who, sadly and regrettably, conclude their best years have been. They won't be disappointed. It is a self-fulfilling prophecy. Our expectancies of our future contribute to our future. Do you believe some of your best years are before you, or do you believe your best years have been?

In Revelation 21:5 we discover these words of grace: "And he who sat upon the throne said, "Behold, I make all things new." God is making all things new in your life. This day.

We learn as much by what the New Testament does *not* say as by what it does say. The text does not say, "And God said, Behold, I make all things old." Regrettably, some think their best days have been. Yes, there were some good days in the past, but not all our best days have been and are over. We have this confidence: God gives us strengths and competencies for the present and future, not simply the past.

The text does not say, "Behold, I make all things the same," as though everything stays starkly the same, from one day, one year to the next. On occasion, we may think it appears as though there is a dreary routineness in life. Yet life is not a never-ending horizon of sameness. We have this confidence: God encourages us to grow and develop our strengths and competencies.

The text does not even say, "you or we make all things new." We are not in this alone, left to our own devices, as though our future depended solely on us, with no resources available to us. Our God is more loving and caring than that. The promise of the Gospel, the good news of God's grace, the compassion of God is that God is moving, stirring, helping in our lives. Know this: God is making all things new in your life. This day. Now. The present and the future are before you. The first step forward is to claim your strengths.

○

God of grace and compassion,
   help us claim the strengths with which You bless our lives.
 Help us not look down on ourselves,
    or think more poorly of ourselves than we have a right to.
      Still our insecurities.
        Quiet our fears.
         Hush our anxieties.
Grant us the confidence and assurance to claim our strengths.
   Help us become new persons. This day.
     Help us sense the stirring, moving, living
      presence of Your Spirit in our lives.
        With assurance in the grace of God, we pray. Amen.

2

POSSIBILITIES FOR A WHOLE, HEALTHY LIFE

KEYS OPEN DOORS. The twelve keys open doors for a whole, healthy life. Sometimes we lock ourselves away from the very possibilities that will give us a rich, full life. These twelve keys help you open the doors to advancing and growing, building and developing your life.

I call these twelve keys "possibilities" because they are, in fact, potential ways you can grow forward. I shy away from referring to them as virtues or values. Those terms raise the specter of "should," "ought," "must," "law." We are the people of grace, not law. These twelve keys are possibilities, generously available to you.

These twelve keys grow out of my own experiences with life. They draw on the wisdom and compassion of the thousands of persons—the mentors, friends, colleagues, and family—who have contributed to my own life's pilgrimage. These possibilities draw on the future and on tradition, hope and common sense, scripture and prayer.

These twelve keys help those of us who seek to live everyday, ordinary life as best we can. They help you develop a whole, healthy life. They apply as well to your family, your work, and the groups in which you participate. Study the book with all four areas in mind—your life, family, work, groups—and you will benefit in all four areas.

Healthy people create healthy families. Healthy families create healthy people. Healthy people create healthy work environments, and healthy work environments create healthy people. Healthy people create healthy groups. Healthy groups create healthy people.

There is a direct correlation between the health of the persons in a group and the health of the group. The more persons in a group who look down on themselves, deny their strengths, suffer from low self-esteem, the more likely the group is to do likewise. The more we, as persons, live strong, healthy lives, the more likely we are to have a group that is whole and healthy.

The more persons in a group who claim their strengths, the more likely the group is to claim its strengths. Groups influence the way we live. Equally important, the way we live influences the health and wholeness of the groups in which we live. The twelve keys are people principles. They help with groups because they focus more on people than on institutions. As people principles, they directly help persons with their lives.

You will discover prayers and responses in this book. These are resources for your prayer and meditation time. I encourage you to read the book both in a good-fun, good-times spirit and, alongside this spirit, to reflect on the twelve keys in a devotional spirit. Draw on the prayers as ways of inspiring and enriching your life and the lives of those around you. At the end of the book, you will discover the Life Possibilities Guides. You are welcome to use these to assess where your current strengths are, and to decide which possibilities you look forward to developing in your own life.

Foundations to Grow

The twelve keys to a whole, healthy life are

mission	joy
compassion	wisdom
hope	encouragement
community	creativity
leadership	health
simplicity	generosity

People teach me that these are the foundations for a happy, productive life. Look at the twelve. In developing your life, see these twelve as foundational, beginning possibilities. There may be possibilities beyond these twelve; there may be fifteen to twenty possibilities that help us with our lives. You are welcome, in the future, to consider a more extensive list. For now, growing some of these twelve keys contributes directly to the richness and fullness of your life. The art of a strong, healthy life is to develop some of the twelve possibilities.

Grow forward the ones that match with

- Your current strengths
- The keys you would have fun advancing
- The direction in which you sense God is inviting you

When you have nine of the twelve keys well in place as strengths, your life will be productive and happy. You will have a sense of peace, productivity, satisfaction, and contentment about your life.

One mistake people make when they look at the chart of these twelve possibilities is to ask, "Do I have all twelve?" That is the old, old friend, a compulsiveness to perfectionism, showing up yet another time in our lives. You do not need all twelve.

Grow those you can grow, at this time in your life. Grow forward where you *can* grow forward, not where you think you *should*. At a different time in life, you might focus on yet another choice. You do not need all twelve to lead a whole, healthy life. It might be interesting to have all twelve. But life is not usually made that way. Not all things are available to us at every point in our life's pilgrimage. Even if all twelve are possible, having them all is not a necessity.

Be at Peace About the Rest

When you have developed nine strengths, two things will happen with the other three keys. The first thing is that the other three won't matter.

A major league baseball player was having a remarkable second season, batting .300 plus, with a goodly number of home runs and runs batted in. He said, "You learn your capabilities, and you learn your limits; you learn how to take what people give you. I'm having fun."[1]

Part of life is developing our strengths; part of life is learning our limits. Develop the nine possibilities that work for you, that are your best capabilities. Now and then, you may find yourself wishing for the other three. Mostly, you will discover that they, initially considered so crucial, have taken on a lesser relative value. Your focus is on the nine that work best for you.

---

[1]John Mabry, St. Louis Cardinals. Reported by Associated Press in the Sunday *Denver Post,* July 28, 1996.

A second thing will happen. I call it spillover impact. The others will come along with a dynamic of their own. We become productive, have fun developing the keys on which we have decided to concentrate. We become more relaxed about the others. We become less tense and tight, nervous and anxious about them. We release our fatal preoccupation with them. Thus, they more naturally flourish alongside those on which we are focusing. To our delight, some of these others seem almost to come along on their own as a result of spillover from the strengths we have grown.

God's Stirring

We discover in Ephesians 2:8 these encouraging words of grace:

> For by grace you have been saved through faith; and this is not your
> own doing, it is the gift of God.

God gives us the gift of life. This is the first wonder: *miracle, extraordinary event*. We live. We breathe. We are alive because God has given us life. God goes further. God gives us these twelve keys, these possibilities, resources, strengths with which to live a rich, full life. This is the second wonder: *marvel, remarkable gift*. We are given both the gift of life and the possibilities with which to develop a whole, healthy life.

God goes even further. God gives us the capacity to grow forward. Not only are we given the gift of life and the possibilities with which to develop our lives, we are given the ability, the capacity to grow and develop in our lives. This is not our own doing. It is the gift of God. This is the third wonder: *benefaction, striking gift*. God goes further. God is present, moving in our lives. God helps us to grow forward our strengths. This is the fourth miracle: *mystery, inexplicable gift*. God is present with you now as you read these words. God is a stirring, living presence in your life this very minute.

> Give thanks to God four times:
>   once, for the gift of your life;
>   second, for the possibilities, the strengths
>   with which God has blessed you;
>   third, for the capacity to grow these
>   possibilities forward in your life's pilgrimage;
>   fourth, for the stirring, moving presence of God's
>   Spirit with you this moment.
> All we are and will be is the gift of God.

○

God of mission and of mystery,
  God of majesty and wonder,
    help us live beyond our low self-esteem.
Still our compulsiveness toward perfectionism.
  Release our anger. Lift our depression.
Grant us wisdom and judgment.
  Give us vision and common sense.
Let our lives be filled with progress and pace,
  prayer and power.
With confidence in the compassion of Christ, we pray. Amen.

3

MISSION

ORVILLE LOVED CHILDREN. That is the simplest, easiest way to describe the mission of this remarkable man. He was principal of the Brady Lake Elementary School and, for years upon years, the most beloved person in the community.

He had a hearty laugh, and wonderful wisdom. He had a marvelous capacity to discern the gentlest ways to encourage children. His encouraging grace freed kids to discover their strengths. He was not tall; he was stocky, balding, most of his hair was gone, and he was on his way to having the build of a wonderful Santa Claus. He was a legend.

The offers came year after year. "We have a bigger school for you." "We have a better school for you." "We have a newer school for you." "There is the promotion to the County Education Office." "We would love for you to move to our county in another part of the state and be our superintendent of schools." Orville stayed.

Brady Lake was a small community of plain, older homes, mostly small, not fancy, gathered around a modest, clear blue lake. People enjoyed reasonable fishing in the summer, the wonderful turning of the trees in autumn, some ice-skating in the winter, the fields coming to new life in the spring. Farms nestled up to the homes. These were old farms, with great barns built on enormous barnstone foundations. The crops came from apple orchards, cornfields, and strawberry patches. Some farms had a few cows. These were unassuming farms, not wealthy farms. They were cared for by plain, decent people.

Orville was content. He knew he had found his mission: the children of Brady Lake. He knew he was in the right place with the right group. He felt led to help these children. He could relate to these kids. He knew what growing up was like in this community. He had discovered his longings and his competencies. He shared concrete, effective help. He lived a life of unconditional service. His help was freely given. Countless lives were helped by this one wise, caring man who went about his quiet and unassuming mission year in and year out.

Longings to Serve

Mission is one key, one possibility, that helps you live a whole, healthy life. You are here for a purpose. Your life does count. God has a plan for your life. God gives you your longings so you can discover purpose for your life. We are whole, healthy persons as we discover and share our longings. We know our lives are counting well. We live more fulfilling lives. We are happier and more at peace.

These resources contribute to a healthy purpose in our lives:

○ Our mission lives out our longings.

○ Our mission matches our competencies.

○ The help we share is freely given, with no strings attached.

○ We share concrete, effective help.

Life is mission. Mission is life. God invites us to a life of serving, not a life of surviving. We are not invited to a life that is self-centered and self-seeking. Amidst the competing attractions of this life, the fleeting flimsies that tempt us, the transitory captivations that abound, we are whole and healthy when we discover a life of mission.

We are drawn to serving as plants are drawn to the sun, as roots to water, as eagles to the sky, as runners to the race. We are put on this earth to help one another. Deeply and fully, we know this is our mission. We find life in our serving. When we are serving others, we are participating in the mission of God.

Life is more than surviving. Yes, we want to survive. That is only natural. We want to serve. That is only natural. Both surviving and serving are part of our being. When the two clash, we sometimes choose survival. More often, we choose serving. Service is stronger than survival. Our deepest longings and yearnings are to serve, not survive.

Sometimes, when we are sick, have the flu, or worse, we feel like dying. All we can think about is just barely surviving. Surviving is the cherished shore for which we are searching as from a sinking raft. Even then, we know that surviving without serving is a deserted island, lonely and lost.

Serving is stronger than surviving. Our survival instincts are strong. Our serving instincts are stronger. When we live life at our best, we live a life of serving. Our identity is in our mission, in our serving. We find our best true self in serving, not surviving. God invites us to a life of service, not a life of survival.

God plants within each human heart longings to help. These longings frequently focus on a specific human hurt and hope. Wherever there is a hurt, there is a hope. Some people discover their longings to help by way of persons wrestling with some form of addiction. Some have longings to help persons with their grieving, having lost a loved one. Some are drawn to helping children living in broken homes. Consider what specific human hurt and hope you may be drawn to help with.

For some persons (and this was Orville), their longings focus on a given stage of life. Orville saw his life's mission to help children during the stage of elementary school. Some are drawn to a mission with preschool children. Some discover their mission with junior high or high school youth. Some have longings to help persons in midlife crisis, or early retirement, or senior adults.

Some people see their mission in helping a particular person who means much to them. A mother, or a father, now ill and bedfast. Many are drawn to a mission of helping their family, in good times and in tragic times. Many see their mission in helping their children and grandchildren develop into constructive adults. Some discover their mission in helping a grouping of persons, frequently an informal network of friends, share whole, healthy lives. Some discover their longings to help those in a given vocation: salespersons, ditch diggers, miners, factory workers, computer scientists, or secretaries. For some, a community interest—such as education, safety, housing, or poverty—stirs their longings to help.

Your longings may lead you to help the addicted. You may be drawn to a mission with preschool families. Your longings may be to raise your children, to help your grandchildren, to assist your parents. Your longings may focus on your helping with a specific vocation. You may be led to help persons with their education. You may have longings to assist the poor.

Barbara had raised three children. She had done good work. They had become solid, healthy persons. She had never planned to raise children again. She discovered Tommy, a young boy with no parents or family. She said she felt she was put on earth to raise this child. She wasn't looking for this mission. She found it.

Bill serves in a slum tenant project, helping elementary school kids find their way. He knows he has found his mission.

Sue is caring for her two grandchildren. Their mother and father were killed in an automobile accident. She talks of the mission that God has given her.

Sometimes, we discover our longings in the midst of daily life. Sometimes, a precipitating event, a celebration, or a crisis stirs our deepest, best longings. Sometimes, it seems our longings find us. We worry about someone, and the hurt with which they are struggling. We lay awake at night, anxious about some person. We look in the mirror in the morning, and our mind keeps going to some person who stirs our heart. We are driving down the road and our thoughts drift to someone, concerned for their well-being. Our worrying, the drifting of our minds, our anxiety for someone are all God's way of teaching us our longings.

God plants people around us who help us discover our longings. One helpful understanding of the parable of the Samaritan suggests the good neighbor is the man in the ditch. Jesus is asked, "Who is the good neighbor?" In response, he shares the parable of the Samaritan.

Who is the good neighbor? The good neighbor is the one who draws forth the best in the other. It is the man in the ditch who drew forth the best in a Samaritan, who, in the centuries come and gone, has been called the Good Samaritan. Sometimes, the person we are helping is really helping us to live our lives at our best. Mission is mutual. It is never quite clear who is really helping whom.

God comes to us as the man in the ditch to stir our longings. God comes to us as the unexpected stranger, a Samaritan, who helps us out of the ditch in which we find ourselves. God comes to us like the innkeeper who tends our wounds and restores us to health. God comes to us in many ways to stir our longings.

We share in God's mission when we help some person or grouping with the wholeness and health of their life. Ask yourself, whom do you long to serve in mission? What specific human hurts and hopes, what life stage, are you drawn to? What persons, family, grouping come to your mind? What vocation draws you? What community interest stirs your heart? Within you, God has planted longings to help.

Competencies to Share Help

We live whole, healthy lives as we discover our longings for a specific mission and our competencies for that mission. God gives us both our longings to serve and matching competencies sufficient unto our longings. Consider what you have fun doing. What you have fun doing is God's way of teaching you your competencies. Consider what you do best. What you do best is God's way of teaching you your mission. We may not have all of the competencies we wish we had. We do have competencies that match the longings God gives us.

We want our lives to count. Oh, not necessarily in any grandiose way. In some simple, enduring way. We want to know that, having lived our lives, our life has had some purpose, has not been lived for nothing. Some people have benefited. Sometimes, we are drawn to the fads of the moment, or become preoccupied with what we can get for ourselves, or are driven by lesser impulses that betray our best true selves. Yet, in the end, we do want our lives to amount to something.

Our helping is grounded in our recognition of a power higher than we ourselves. Our service is grounded in God. We love because God first loves us. We discover whose we are. We are no longer afraid. We act in mission because of who and whose we are, and as we serve we become more fully who and whose we already are. Jesus said, "Be not afraid" (John 6:20 KJV). These are freeing words. We let go the tense tightness, the nervous anxiousness. We worry less for our survival. We are less preoccupied with success. The things of this world take on their relative, proper priority. We are freed to serve.

The art of life is to discover one's mission. The joy of life is to serve well. To serve well means guarding against having too many missions, too many ways of serving, at one time. When we do that we defuse our energies, scatter our competencies, and do too little in too many directions. It is for nought, to rush hither and yon. To serve poorly is to lessen the richness of life. To serve too many missions at one time is to lessen the fullness of life. It is helpful to focus one's mission.

We may discover more than one mission in our lifetime. You may sense that your mission—for now—is raising your children. To a certain extent, it is a lifelong mission. They are your children even when they are older. It becomes important, then, to treat them as adults. At the same time, there comes a point when the primary nature of that mission—raising one's children—is fulfilled, and whatever remains of that mission is secondary. Another mission may then become primary. For some, it may now be caring for their aged parents. Whatever the mission, God gives you the ability to grow the competencies forward to match the mission for each moment in your life.

We share our service in prayerful ways. As we share help, there is a spirit of prayer about what we do, a quiet realization of the nearness of God in our lives. A profound sense of serving gives a profound sense of living in the presence of God, of being surrounded by the grace and love of God, of being led forward by the power and hope of God. The deeper the prayer, the richer the helping. Serving is an act of prayer, an act of reverence and communion with God. Sense, in your life, the living, moving, stirring presence of God.

We serve the God of the galaxies. God invites us to the twenty-first century. God goes before us as a cloud by day and a fire by night. The stars, the galaxies, the universe are before us. Live a life of prayer, more deeply than you ever have. This is a time for silent reverence. This is a time for prayerful service and deep compassion, not pretentious predictions and foolish forecasts. God leads us toward that future which God has promised and prepared for us. The whispering soul of prayer will see us into the future.

We have a hushed, desperate, foundational life search for individuality: for identity, integrity, autonomy, and power, in the midst of the dislocation and displacement of power of our times. We search for community: for roots, place, and belonging, as older forms of community are scattered across the landscape. We have a profound search for meaning: for value, purpose, and significance for our lives, amidst the confused, chaotic array of meanings that abound. We search for hope: for some reliable, certain view of the future, even as the older order of things passes away. We find and fulfill these foundational life searches as we discover our longings and share our competencies.

Our Help Is Freely Given

We live whole, healthy lives as our help is freely given. Do you remember being given a gift with strings attached? The person giving the gift was well meaning. But there were conditions and stipulations. The gift was a trap. It had strings: requirements and provisions. It was not freely given. Sometimes, we have given gifts with strings attached. In effect, we have implied, or even said out loud, "I will give you this, but you must therefore do such and such." Sometimes people have openly said to us, "I will give you this on condition that you do such and such."

God teaches us well. God's grace is freely given. There is nothing we can do to earn the grace of God. There is nothing we can do to manipulate the grace of God. While our lives are yet in disarray, God initiates the sharing of grace with us—a most remarkable gift, generously given—with no strings attached.

With the gift of the grace of God, for us the day of striving is over. The day of serving has come. Amazed at the generosity of God's gift of grace, we become less interested in what we can get and more interested in what we can give. We develop the awareness that persons need our help now. We discover the sense that our serving is a gift of grace.

We become less preoccupied with the distractions of this life, the gridlock of meetings, the desks stacked high with papers, the calendars filled with busy appointments. The determined driving toward success, whatever that might mean, the rush of the days and the weeks, the declining sense of value and worth in life, these are no more. That way of living life becomes less functional. Getting and grabbing are done. Striving simply sputters and stumbles to a stop. For us, it no longer works.

We have the confidence the mission we are sharing is freely given. There is a sense of urgency to our serving. We have discovered a rich sense of mission. We share sound wisdom and judgment, strong vision and common sense. We are living a deep, full life of prayer. We live with a spirit of compassion, a sense of community, and a spirit of hope. God shares with us a joyful invitation: to serve in mission.

We are always at our best in a life of mission. Do not long for the return of an older time. The hurried business, the frantic labors, the driving determination, all of these efforts to succeed in getting and grabbing for us have come to nothing. This is not where we are at our best. When we serve in mission, that is where we are lean and strong, have courage and compassion. In that older time we became bloated and bureaucratic, busy and stressful. In mission we are at our blazing best.

In mission we live best what some call the parable of the lost sheep. I call it the parable of the good shepherd. It tells a whole lot more about the shepherd who is good than about the sheep. What the sheep did was get lost. The good shepherd is the one who leaves the ninety-nine gathered in the wilderness. Note that even the ninety-nine are not gathered at a barn. In Matthew 18:12, they are on the hills. In Luke 15:4, they are in the wilderness. The good shepherd runs to the one lost in the rough, rocky places of life. Our predicament—indeed, I think it is the promise of our times—is that because the vast majority of people are in need of help, we have been given an amazing mission field.

In an earlier time, we might have been timid and cautious, preoccupied and busy with our own success, whatever that may mean. We sometimes behaved like Little Bo Peep. We waited. Our motto was, "Leave them alone and they'll come home, wagging their tails behind them." The notion that God invites us to sit, waiting for people to find us, is wishfulness, a lazy indifference, a slothful egotism. We have discovered the way God relates to us, living with us at the front lines of our lives. We have discovered God's freely given, fully initiated, proactive grace with us, and we do likewise with persons in need of help.

A good shepherd is at the front lines of people's human hurts and hopes. Three things are true of any M*A*S*H team: there is a shortage of personnel, there are inadequate supplies, there is hardly enough of anything. With compassion and creativity, a M*A*S*H team delivers competent medical care. Serving in God's mission, we experience a shortage of personnel, inadequate supplies, and hardly enough of anything. Yet we deliver competent missional care in people's lives and destinies.

We may have a tent. We do not need a fort. We are more like a pilgrimage people. Our sense of permanence is our compassion for mission, not our commitment to mortar. Our permanence is sharing the sacrament of serving, not our commitment to some system. What is needed, in our time, are good shepherd mission teams who run to persons who have specific human hurts and hopes and deliver real and effective help.

We are not alone. God gives us our longings, our competencies, and persons who have matching longings and competencies. In our midst are people with whom we can share. The text ". . . where two or three are gathered . . ." (Matt. 18:20) affirms two things: first, there are two or three who can gather with you, and second, Christ is fully present with you.

In *Chariots of Fire,* the great British runner sits in the stands, stunned, shocked at having just been soundly beaten in a race. He says to his lady friend sitting beside him, "I won't run if I can't win." His lady friend says back, "If you don't run, you can't win."

Some people say, "I won't run to persons in need if I can't help them." Ah, good friend, you can't help them if you don't run to them. Run to the mission field. As we move into the twenty-first century, run to the mission field. Freely share your help. God is encouraging you with grace. God is blessing your life.

Concrete, Effective Help

We live whole, healthy lives as we share concrete, effective help. The art of helping is to deliver almost enough help to be helpful, but not so much help that the help becomes harmful and creates a pattern of codependency. We are encouraged to share more than simply good intentions, or glowing generalities, or pious platitudes. There is more to helping than well-meaning lectures and legalisms.

Yet concrete, effective help is not heavy-handed help, nor the wrong kind of help, nor too much help. Well-intentioned people, in their desire to be helpful, sometimes deliver too much help. They think they are helping but their help is harming. They take on themselves the whole effort, blocking the recipient from participating in the helping process. The art is to encourage a spirit of self-reliance and self-sufficiency, so people can work through their hurt and hope.

The art is to share the help that really helps. The Good Samaritan gave help that was fitting. There was no lecture. There were no conditions. He simply shared what was needed in the moment. The innkeeper, likewise, gave just enough help that the man could be on his way. There is nothing in the text to suggest the man lived with the innkeeper for the rest of his days. That would have been codependency. There was just enough help given that the man could continue his journey.

This way of serving is an art, inviting prayer and discernment, learning and growth, wisdom and compassion. The ancient injunction "If you cannot do good, at least do no harm" has wisdom. Sometimes, we mistakenly deliver the help we think they should have, or we mistakenly deliver the help they think they need. The art is to avoid delivering the wrong kind of help, or too much help.

God invites us to solid, strong self-esteem, not low self-esteem. Solid self-esteem comes in serving. Those who say we are motivated by survival are wrong. They overlook all the people who in simple ways, in daily life, give their lives in service to help their family, their friends, and their community, all of humankind. They overlook everyone who, in heroic ways, in times of peace, and in times of crisis, lay down their lives for friends, family, even strangers. We sacrifice to serve.

Life is more than being scared and scarred. People are not stingy and selfish. Some persons are scared. Persons and events in their lives have scared them. They have become anxious, frightened. They find themselves abiding in panic and fear. Some have been so damaged by events and persons that they carry the sad scars of those awful times. Abandonment and abuse abound. The memories of their miseries are terrifying. They have been scarred. Some persons have been both scared and scarred. The symptoms, stingy and selfish, are self-protective measures. They do not want to be scared or scarred again.

We have all been scared and scarred to some extent. Life brings us these experiences. When we discover our longings for mission, longings that are a deeper part of our being, and when we discover our competencies, which are God's gift to us, our longings and our competencies overcome our scaredness and scarredness. We live forward to our best, true selves.

Life is more than self-seeking and self-centered striving. Life is more than the bigger house, the better car, or the next promotion. Our identity is in our mission, not in some job we have with a company. In an earlier culture (and still sometimes in the present culture) a question frequently asked was, "What do you do?" The culture equated who we are with what we do. Identity was job. The message was, "You are your job."

Sometimes, we have fallen into that trap as well. We are more than a job. As important or as mundane as our work may be—and sometimes it is both—who we are is more than the job we currently have. We will likely have more than one job across our lifetime. Sometimes, we take new jobs because we grow and develop. Our interests and abilities advance and build, and we discover new possibilities, and thus fresh and distinctive jobs. Sometimes, downsizing and retrenchment force us into new jobs.

What is true in life is this: "Be loyal to God, and God will be loyal to you. Be unloyal to God, and God will still be loyal to you." God does not forsake us when we forsake God. God is loyal with us. The one, certain, eternal truth is that God's love and grace, God's peace and hope endure.

The old admonition to be loyal to the company and the company will be loyal to you, that ancient mantra, is an illusion. In recent times, people have found out how empty that promise is. People no longer trust institutions or businesses to fulfill that promise. It is a hollow, empty promise.

Some people, having spent their whole lives in a given institution, are now caught in a double bind. On the one hand, they know the promise is hollow. They might be dismissed any day. Their job might be gone in one fleeting moment, as a fragment of dust before the wind. On the other hand, they have wrapped up so much of their identity in the job and the institution that they continue to fight for its survival. They try to protect the institution they helped build because their identity is in that institution. What they are really doing is fighting for the survival of their own identity. If the institution were to die, they would no longer have a job. They believe that were the institution to die, they would die. Their sense of identity would die with it.

Life develops new purpose, value, and significance as we discover and share our mission. Life is more than a job. Our identity is not in a job. Jobs come and go, wither and fade. We may have several in the course of our lives. Our identity is not in some institution or business. That way of achieving identity no longer works. It is an illusion. The meaning of life is in the mission.

Our identity is not in status in the culture. The notion that the purpose of life is to achieve higher status in the culture is a hollow notion. When we achieve status, we enjoy the perks, prestige, and prerogatives. Many are driven to do better, to be better thought of, to travel in circles of culture and prestige. When people attain higher status in the culture, they discover how empty it is. They enjoy it, with a smile on their faces. Yet, there is an emptiness in their heart and soul. It is not all they thought it would be. It does not bring the satisfaction and peace, contentment and serenity they thought it would.

Moreover, who is on top today may be near the bottom tomorrow. Institutions are here now and then gone. Organizations flourish and shrivel. Our identity is not finally in the customs, habits, and traditions of a particular culture. Civilizations ascend and diminish. Establishments come and go. Denominations whither and fade. Jobs and professions disappear; some vanish overnight.

The mission of God is eternal. We see beyond the fragile foolishness, the momentary superficialities around us. What lasts is our service. What lasts is concrete, effective help. What has abiding, enduring value is the mission we share, which touches people's lives and shapes their destinies. What lasts is not so much a place. What lasts are people, who live richer and fuller lives because they have discovered their longings and competencies, and freely give their help.

Is your life counting in some enduring way? When you are serving others, you are participating in the mission of God. The question of the culture, "What do you do?" has usually been answered with a description of our job. The deeper search in our lives, sometimes not consciously realized, is the question of mission.

In *Star Wars*, the phrase is, "The Force be with you." There is a force permeating the universe, surrounding us, strengthening us. For the whole, healthy person, the phrase is, "The mission of God be with you." God's mission permeates the universe, surrounding us, strengthening us, leading us forward. When we participate in the mission of God, we participate in the primary force of the universe, to which the heavens and the galaxies attest and bear witness. The very firmament testifies to the mission of God.

With our longings and our competencies, we freely share concrete, effective help.

> For I was hungry and you gave me food,
> I was thirsty and you gave me drink,
> I was a stranger and you welcomed me,
> I was naked and you clothed me,
> I was sick and you visited me,
> I was in prison and you came to me. (Matt. 25:35–36)

God gives us the gift of our longings to help, matching competencies, the ability to freely give, and the capacity to share our help. We grow as we serve. We live as we share. Mission is the breath of life.

—————— o ——————

God invites us to mission.

    We are the people of mission and service.

God plants within each human heart longings to help.

    We are thankful for the gift of our longings.

God gives competencies sufficient unto the mission.

    We are grateful for the competencies with which God blesses us.

God freely gives to us the richness of grace and help.

    We freely give of our longings and competencies. They are gifts of God.

God helps us share concrete, effective help.

    With our whole lives, we give thanks to God. Amen.

4

COMPASSION

JULIE'S GROUP OF QUILTING FRIENDS meets monthly. They share fellowship and are resources for one another in their interest in quilting. They are a remarkable group, among the most helpful in the area. When one of the members was hospitalized for surgery, the group voted to send flowers. Since they had a small treasury at the time, they limited the expenditure to ten dollars. So the florist delivered a glass vase with three flowers in it.

Julie later visited the ailing friend and was disappointed by the vase with the three flowers. Quietly, she resolved to find a better way for the group to express its concern and compassion if another member were to have a serious injury or illness.

Her research turned up a patchwork quilt block of a basket of flowers. When the officers met next, she presented a plan, which was quickly adopted. Volunteers made the quilt blocks using bright fabric scraps for the flowers. The patchwork was incorporated into covers for throw pillows, and the treasury paid the modest expense for the pillows.

Months passed. One day a member fell and broke a bone in her foot. A flower basket pillow was inscribed with a message wishing a speedy recovery, and Julie took it to the homebound friend, stayed for a brief visit, then left. Over the next two years, six flower basket pillows were shared with members on behalf of the group.

The recipients have been so touched by the expression of sharing and caring that they have wanted to help make more pillow covers. More than that, they have found other ways they can use their sewing skills to share compassion in the community. They are making baby quilts for the local pregnancy center, and some have begun making gowns for the local hospice patients.

Quietly and gently, Julie has helped me learn much about compassion. Most acts of compassion have a quiet generosity about them. Compassion

is gracious and gentle, not loud and noisy. Compassion does not call attention to itself. Compassion is direct and simple. Compassion is not boisterous. Compassion is not harsh and demanding. Compassion shares love and
kindness, generously and thoughtfully.

Julie has shared remarkable compassion in raising our children. She has
shared her compassion with the vast numbers of persons with whom she
worked in the medical school of Emory University. She has shared many
acts of compassion with the countless groups we have helped across the
years. I am again and again amazed at her resources of compassion. Her
whole life is a testimony of compassion.

My greatest gift is simply to be Julie's husband. In the area where we
spend much of our time, Julie is known for her contributions in several
groups. The quilting group is among the strongest groups in the area.
With my speaking and travel schedule, she is there more than I am. With
her activities, she is well known in the area. Frequently, when I meet someone, they will say, with considerable delight, "Oh, you're Julie's husband."
To be "Julie's husband" is the deepest, richest honor in this journey.

God shares compassion directly. God sends persons to us with whom
we discover the full meaning of compassion. I am most grateful for all I
have learned and discovered about compassion from Julie McCoy Callahan. Her sense of humility, her sharing and being with people, her deep
love for them, her sense of forgiveness, generous and full, all these have
helped me understand the richness and fullness of compassion.

Consider the people God has given to you, with whom you have discovered—and continue to discover—the rich, full depth of compassion.

A Steady, Quiet Humility

One key, one possibility, for a whole, healthy life is compassion. God
invites us to a life of compassion. We are at our best when, amidst the difficulties, the resentments, the bitterness, the grudges that abound, we discover these resources:

○ Compassion begins with humility.

○ Compassion includes sharing and being with people.

○ Compassion is a deep love for people.

○ Compassion involves forgiveness.

The deeper the humility, the fuller the compassion. Humility is the beginning of compassion. When we have humility, we no longer focus on
ourselves. Our own ego needs lessen. We no longer see ourselves as the

center of the universe. We can focus with other persons. There is no compassion without steady, quiet humility.

People with solid self-esteem have the confidence and assurance to have humility. People with low self-esteem are frequently too preoccupied with themselves and thus have difficulty focusing on the other person with love and compassion. People who are *searching for* compassion sometimes have difficulty *sharing* compassion. They are seeking to shore up their low self-esteem. As a result, they are too involved with themselves.

People who have experienced expressions of compassion know they are truly loved. They are quietly awed by the generous gift of compassion. They are humbled by the compassion shared with them. They develop solid self-esteem, confidence, and assurance; they richly share compassion. It is interesting that the persons of history whom we admire most for their compassion are people of deep humility.

People with low self-esteem frequently complain, whine, bemoan, and lament about this or that. Whatever people focus on becomes their habit. When they "give away" complaining, share complaining with those around them, this complaining pattern tragically becomes stronger in them. When, on the other hand, they keep their complaining to themselves, it becomes weaker and finally disappears. Like muscles when not used, it atrophies and decays. Moreover, if we keep our complaining to ourselves, we aren't able to put up with it, and we finally decide life is better without our complaining.

Whatever you give away becomes stronger. Whatever you keep becomes weaker. With humility, give away your compassion. It becomes stronger. As you share your love and affection with those around you, your compassion "strength" becomes stronger. Keep your compassion to yourself and it becomes weaker and finally disappears. One's own ego, one's own self is not finally the environment where compassion thrives best. Give your compassion away. It will flourish and grow.

We have seen compassion expressed by a teacher who senses the pain and struggle of particular students, and who quietly offers some key piece of help that boosts them over a particular hurdle. We have seen compassion expressed by a passing motorist who stops to give help by changing the flat tire of a stranded young mother. A young high school student shares acts of compassion by going next door and clearing the snow off the sidewalk of her elderly neighbor before she leaves for school. Freely offered, these compassionate acts have no expectation of reward. One person senses a need of another and humbly offers an act of help and kindness.

Our time is a time for humility. The waters ahead are deep and uncharted. We go where humankind has never gone before. We do not need to become arrogant and prideful. What does not help is to develop an egocentrism of the historical moment. Regrettably, some persons have, on occasion, acquired vain self-righteousness. They fancy that it is their fateful, awesome responsibility to lead humankind into the twenty-first century. These are but the whims of mortals, blown astray by the winds of ego and pride, fear and anxiety.

What is needed for this moment in history is humility. The noisy clang of pride, the tinkling sound of ego, the hollow footfall of self-righteousness, these do not help. What helps is the quiet, steady humility of God's servants. This is a time for thoughtful examination. We are not worthy of the trust placed in our hands.

We are sinful. We have fallen short of the glory of God. We have loved our own creations too much. We have aspired too much. We have confused our own success with God's mission. We stand in rich, full need of God's forgiveness. Humility helps us share compassion.

Sharing and Being with People

One cannot express compassion in isolation. It is not a principle, discussed and debated in a vacuum. The only way we can express or experience compassion is as we share with one another. The teacher expressed compassion; the student experienced it. The motorist expressed compassion; the stranded young mother experienced it. Alexandria expressed compassion; her elderly neighbor experienced it.

This sharing is not boisterous, noisy; the glad hand, the hard slap on the back; not the life of the party. Neither is it retreating into a shell, isolated and insulated from human contact; withdrawn into self. Many people who enjoy sharing are quiet, gentle, and shy persons. God blesses quiet, shy persons. You can enjoy being with people, and do so quietly and gently. Sometimes, we share an expression of compassion as we walk through the valley of the shadow. Tragedy visits us. Sickness stands at our bedside. Sudden events of sadness surround us. We draw closer to one another. We share the sense of our presence and comfort. We know we are one.

Our sharing may happen as we gather to celebrate a birthday, happy and joyous. It is grand to be together. Often, the sharing takes place as two people sit side by side, hushed and happy, watching the sun set. They have shared a good day together. Indeed, the sharing is frequently quiet, respectful. It is gentle, almost reverent. Two people, or more, have the privilege of sharing and being with one another. There is a sacramental spirit to the sharing. For that one tender, precious moment, they are one.

A Deep Love for People

Humility, sharing, and a deep love for people are the ancestors of compassion. With a sense of humility, we share and enjoy being with people. In doing so, we discover a deeper, richer love for them. There is wisdom in love, and folly in not loving. As we discover a deep love for people, we discover the richness and fullness of life. We see the colors of life, the light and sun of the day, and the stars of the heavens. The folly in not loving is that life becomes gray and dull, the day dark and gloomy.

A compassion for people includes loving persons for who they are, not for who we hope they could be. A deep love for persons does not seek to remake them into someone else. When we share this quality of love with a person, there are no legalisms and laws, conditions and stipulations. This is not a relationship of shoulds and oughts, mandates and demands. It is not conditional.

A deep love for people is a living, moving tenderness and kindness. There is an enthusiasm to share life with the other person. Indifference and cruelty are done away with. Severity and hatred are set aside. There is a spirit of mercy, charity, and generosity. The relationship is one of mutual loving and living, sharing and caring, giving and serving.

Take a moment and recall three persons who, in your own life, have shared with you a deep love. Their relationship with you was one of tenderness and kindness, sharing and caring. Most likely, you think of persons whose love was freely given, unconditional, a gift. There was no hook, no gimmick, no expectation, no payback expected. The love was a gift. Share that same deep love with persons around you. Your own sense of compassion will grow and overflow.

Your compass is your compassion. Follow your heart; then your head. Let your heart rule your head. Reason without love is barren. There is no life. Love gives life to reason. When head rules heart, reason is lonely. When heart rules head, life is full and rich.

When you discover your compassion, you discover God's compassion. When you discover God's compassion, you discover your compassion. Your compassion is one way in which God helps you discover His compassion for you. God's compassion is one way in which He seeks to help you grow your compassion.

Forgiving Generously and Fully

We were sailing that year in the Bahamas, Julie and I and our five- and seven-year-old sons. We had a wonderful sailboat we had chartered. We were having a grand time.

Late one afternoon, a storm came up. The seas began to roll and rise. We learned over the shortwave that, far off, a hurricane was swirling. We were getting the fringe effect from the hurricane. The seas became uncomfortably high, choppy, rough. We headed toward a deserted island—a "key," they call them in the Bahamas. According to the map, there was a small harbor where we could anchor our boat and be protected from the storm.

Near dusk, we made our way into the little harbor of the deserted island. The island was smaller than the map made it appear, and there was a huge coral reef toward the back and on one side of the harbor. We set our anchor to ride out the storm that night. The little bit of beach and island did block the waves from us. It was comparatively comfortable. We settled in.

It wasn't too long before the boat began to drift toward the coral reef. The anchor had slipped. We pulled the anchor up, repositioned the boat with the inboard motor, dropped the anchor on what we thought would be firmer bottom, and began to make preparations for the night. Not too much later, the anchor slipped again. We set it again.

As we went to bed that night, we decided to stand watch so that, should the anchor slip yet another time, we would not find ourselves on the coral reef. So here were a five-year-old and a seven-year-old, Julie, and I taking turns at watch that night. The anchor did slip several times. I would be awakened, if it was not my watch. We would set the anchor and it would last for a while. Then, we would have to set it again.

In the morning, after a nearly sleepless night, we could see that the storm out in the ocean was continuing in its fury. The storm was not going anywhere, nor were we.

The harbor clearly had a soft bottom and anchors would not hold, so I decided to do what is sometimes done, namely carry the anchor to shore, carry it up the beach a ways, dig it deep into the beach, and then it would hold.

Julie had the inboard motor going slowly, just moving us forward. I was standing on the bow of the boat, holding this huge anchor in my arms, looking down into the water. It was clear. The water in the Bahamas is so clear you can see almost forever.

I stepped off into what I thought was shallow water. Halfway down, it dawned on me that if I let go of the anchor I would probably quit sinking. It came to me that the only one in trouble was me. The anchor was safely secured to the boat by a chain and a line. I was the one in trouble. I finally let go the anchor and quit sinking.

That event has occasioned a saying in our family, to be, I am sure, passed down from one generation to the next: "If you want to sink fast, be sure to hold on to an anchor."

Let go. Now, I know, in one sense, God is our anchor. I also know we all carry around with us quiet grudges, deep resentments, hushed bitterness, low-grade hostility, subliminal anger, and occasional eruptive forms of rage. All these weigh us down. As long as we carry them around with us, we continue sinking in this life. Let them go.

Ships are meant for sailing, not for being at anchor. We are meant for sailing, not for allowing ourselves to be pulled down by the anchors we carry around with us.

Paraphrasing Hebrews 12:1, "So then, surrounded as we are with such a great cloud of witnesses all about us, *let us lay aside every weight, encumbrance, impediment, and the sin that so weighs us down,* and let us run steadily the course set before us. . . ."

God invites us to lay aside our resentments, grudges, and bitterness. They only weigh us down. They cause us to sink. With God's help, we lay them aside and run well the race God gives us.

Four resources are available to you as you generously, fully, forgive persons who have wronged you, harmed you, injured you, with whom you have a grudge, hatred, resentment, hostility:

- Accepting God's forgiveness
- Accepting others' forgiveness
- Forgiving oneself
- Forgiving others

These four resources are dynamic, not sequential. As you discover one, the other three come into being. Do the one you can do for this moment. With God's help, and the help of your mentors and friends, grow the one forward that you can do something with, now.

We forgive because God first forgives us. We learn forgiveness as we discover and receive God's forgiveness. In forgiving us, God accomplishes two things: first, forgiving us, and second, teaching us how to forgive. In God's compassion, we discover forgiveness, reconciliation, and restoration. We discover grace and love. Our weak sins and our terrible sins are forgiven.

We forgive because other people forgive us. The gift of their forgiveness is amazing and unconditional. We learn forgiveness as we discover and accept the forgiveness of loved ones, friends, even strangers who forgive us.

Forgive yourself. God does.

Forgive yourself. Others do.

A healthy way to forgive other people is to discover and accept the forgiving love of God, the forgiving love of other persons who share with you.

Sometimes, we become preoccupied with another person's wrong toward us. This is our way to avoid the full extent of our own wrong. By centering on their wrong to us, we seek to avoid seeing the wrongs we have done. This pulls us down, becomes unhealthy for our lives.

Sometimes, we are reluctant to accept forgiveness. We know doing so would invite us to forgive those who have harmed and injured us. How could we accept forgiveness but not also forgive? We imagine that if we can hold at bay God's forgiveness and the other person's forgiveness, then we do not need to forgive those who have injured us.

God's forgiveness is so compelling, so loving that it wins through our every resistance. We discover the wonderful, extraordinary, almost inexpressible way in which God forgives us and invites us to be whole. I think of this as: blessed are they who can forgive themselves, for they shall find peace. God forgives us. Frequently, others forgive us. Many times, the persons we have grievously wronged forgive us. We can forgive generously and fully.

When we do not forgive ourselves, we do these things: we reject God's forgiving compassion, we reject the forgiveness others share with us, we set ourselves above God and those who have forgiven us, and we do not forgive those who have harmed us.

There is a fifth thing: we have no peace.

When we forgive ourselves, we accept God's forgiveness and others' forgiveness. We have peace. God's peace and grace; they comfort us. Forgiving a stranger is easier than forgiving the ones we love the most. Forgiving the ones we love the most is hard because it requires forgiving a deeper sense of betrayal.

Forgiving oneself is harder yet because we know we have betrayed our best true self. We know we have not lived forward in strong, healthy ways. To forgive is to affirm and claim that deep betrayal. As long as we do not forgive, we can pretend the betrayal did not happen. The illusion that we did not sin continues, and that very illusion, that very self-deception, becomes the deeper sin and betrayal.

Meister Eckhart, a teacher of the Middle Ages, had a saying: "The devil has a device called busyness with which he tries to convince Christians they are really doing the will of God."

I add to his thought: "The devil has a device called resentment and bitterness with which he tries to keep Christians from the forgiveness of God."

Forgive.

Compassion Runs

In Luke 15:20, we read: "his father saw him and had compassion, and ran. . . ." Forgiveness runs, generously, fully. Reconciliation runs. Compassion is the food of the soul. Grow your compassion. Compassion does not walk. Compassion runs.

The good news of the text is: "But while he [the young son] was yet at a distance, his father saw him and had *compassion,* and *ran* and embraced him and kissed him. . . . The father said to his servants, 'Bring quickly the best robe, and put it on him; and put a ring on his hand, and shoes on his feet; and bring the fatted calf and kill it, and let us eat and make merry; for this my son was dead, and is alive again; he was lost, and is found'" (Luke 15:20, 22–24).

The far country to which we sometimes carry ourselves is the kingdom of deep resentments, quiet grudges, hushed bitternesses. It is not a pleasant place. It is a pigsty, muck and mud, where we wallow in our own resentments and grudges.

What you can count on and depend upon is this: God runs to you with compassion.

While you are yet a long way off, God runs to you. God does not wait. God does not walk. God runs. God welcomes you home. God throws loving arms around you, and calls for the robe and the ring, the sandals, and to kill the fatted calf; because you who were dead are now alive; you who were lost are now found.

The text is grace, not law.

Regrettably, sometimes you and I write the gospel text in a rules-and-regulations, conditions-and-stipulations, legalistic way. Even with loved ones, friends, family, we sometimes write the text this way:

> While the young son was yet a long way off, the father saw him, and he remembered their last bitter parting. He remembered hearing the inheritance had been squandered in a far country. So he waited in the house until the young son drew nigh. He did not move. The young son knocked once. The father waited. A second time the young son knocked. The father did not move. He waited in the house. A third time the young son knocked. Finally, the father rose and went slowly to the door.
>
> He opened the door, and his son fell on his knees and said, "Father, I have sinned against heaven and before thee. I am no longer worthy to be called thy son. Take me back as one of thy hired servants."
>
> There was a long silence.

Finally, the father said, "Well, who is this? Do I know you? Come in. We will have a long, long talk, one like we used to have. If I am to take you back, there will be ninety-seven conditions and stipulations, policies and procedures, rules and regulations; and if, after five years of dutiful and faithful commitment, you break yea not a single one, I may then yet call you my son."

Good friends, we sometimes do this, yea, even with loved ones, family, friends.

What the gospel text says is: the good news is, while the young son was yet a long way off, his father saw him, and had compassion, and ran to him and welcomed him home. "I love you." Three of the most helpful, hopeful words we will ever hear. To you, God says, "I love you."

God runs to you with compassion. God invites you to run with compassion. God welcomes you home with compassion. God invites you to welcome home friends, loved ones, strangers with compassion. The time to wait is over. The time to run has come. Run well, with compassion.

———————— o ————————

God of all that is here and all that is beyond,
　　stir our passion. Deepen our compassion.
May Your grace be to us a drenching rain of new life.
　　May Your compassion be with us like the rising sun.
　　　　May we sense the living, moving, stirring presence
　　　　of Your forgiveness with us now.
May we receive Your forgiveness.
　　Help us forgive.
　　　　Help us live lives rich with compassion.
　　　　In the name of Christ, we pray. Amen.

5

HOPE

IN THE MIDDLE OF THE NIGHT, our phone rang. At the other end of the line, Mary was confused, upset, babbling, blurting disconnected sentences, near hysteria. I could hardly understand what she was saying.

As best I could make it out, her husband had come home. Words were exchanged. Pushing and shoving occurred. He began beating her. She broke away and locked herself in the bedroom, made a hurried call. Would I come?

I was naïve in those days and said yes. (Today, in comparably desperate circumstances, I am naïve still and say yes still.) There was some considerable credibility to the desperation of her plea because I could hear this banging in the background, as though someone were knocking on or breaking down a bedroom door.

It took me ten minutes to get to the road on which they lived. As I turned down the road, the thing that struck me the most—I can see it now—was pitch darkness. Not a light on anywhere up or down that road: not a street light, not a front yard light, not a porch light, not a light on in any house, save the house toward which I was headed. And, early that morning, every light in the house must have been on.

There was fog, and you know how the light shimmers out across a fog. It gave me a kind of eerie feeling as I parked my car and rushed to the door. The closer I got to the half-open front door, the less interested I was in achieving the door. I could hear hollering and yelling, screaming and shouting in the back of the house.

I did the wise, sensible thing that any competent minister would do under those desperate circumstances. I rang the doorbell. I rang it again. Surely these people would hear their doorbell, interrupt whatever they are doing in the back of the house, and come gently, politely, decently to answer the bell and say, "Why, Pastor, what a delight that you are sharing a pastoral visit with us at two in the morning."

They would invite me in for coffee or tea. We would have a pleasant twenty-minute visit, and I would never have to be a part of whatever mess was going on in their lives early that morning. I was so confident of that strategy that I knocked on the doorjamb. Maybe they hadn't heard the bell. I couldn't knock on the door standing half-ajar. If I had knocked on it, I would have knocked it back against the wall. So I knocked on the doorjamb.

Then, much to my horror and dismay, I found my feet carrying me down the hall toward the noise. I said to my feet, "Let's go back and try that doorbell one more time. Sometimes you have to push them really hard."

I went down the hall, turned to the right, then back to the left, and entered their family room. I just followed the shouting to know where they were.

Mary was strewn across the couch, her night dress torn, blood streaming from the side of her mouth, bruises black and blue beginning to appear on her face. She was indeed having a hard morning.

Her husband was standing over by the fireplace, shouting and yelling, screaming and hollering, making noise that reached to the high heavens, filling that room with more anger, hatred, and hostility than likely all of us could muster in a year's time.

He turned to see what stranger had walked into his own home in the middle of the night. They were not members of our church. They were newcomers in our community. One afternoon, late, I had visited to welcome them as part of the community. Mary had been there. He had not been there.

My custom with newcomer families across the years has been to invite them to put my phone number on the front of their telephone directory. That is where most newcomers keep track of phone numbers they would almost like to remember but cannot quite, yet. I would rather be the penciled phone number on the front of the phone directory than the institutional calling card, now on the dresser, then on the ironing board, and lost a week later.

For whatever reasons, when Mary broke away from her husband, headed into the bedroom, closed and locked the bedroom door, and rushed to the phone, rather than calling the police, she had seen that penciled phone number and called me. He and I had never met.

When he turned to see what stranger had just walked into his home amidst the chaos and confusion he was creating, I noticed for the first time he was holding in his arm, just the way John Wayne used to hold those things in the movies, he was holding in his arm a semiautomatic submachine gun.

There was in me, in one split second, an eternity of terror. I can feel it now.

There was also a side of me that said, "By golly, he doesn't use that for deer hunting. He probably doesn't use it for duck hunting. He wouldn't use it for target shooting. He would obliterate the targets."

I am a reasonably wise, sensible person. It dawned on me as I stood there in sheer terror that what I said next might very well be decisive for me, and for Mary—and, I learned later, for three little kids huddled in a back bedroom, their door closed, sort of tucked under their bed, wondering what in the name of heaven mommy and daddy were doing early that morning, and not very interested in finding out.

I said, "John. . . ." And I caught him just a little.

As best I can in this life's pilgrimage, I believe in living it through with people on a first-name basis. In that hurried, confused, near-hysteria telephone call, Mary had described her husband, John, as having come home and beating her. Since it sounded like he and I were at last going to meet, I had remembered his name.

Here was John seeing a total stranger, walking into his own home early that morning, amidst all of the disturbance and commotion he was creating, and calling him by his first name. I caught his attention just a little.

I said, "John, where are you headed? What kind of future are you building this morning?" Those two questions caught John just long enough that we could begin a four-hour conversation that eventuated in a five-year relationship as John and Mary and their three kids, myself, and a host of others helped them to build forward a rich and full future.

John had come home from his own fair share of carousing and carrying-on. He had found his wife, Mary, in her own fair share of carousing and carrying-on. The neighbor had gotten away. Out of his guilt over what he had been about, and out of his anger over what he had found in his home, and most especially out of his terror, he had been shouting to the high heavens.

Terror. Take away a person's memories, and he becomes anxious. Take away a person's hopes, and he becomes terrified. When John walked into his own home early that morning and found what he found, whatever hopes he had for himself, whatever hopes he had for himself and Mary, whatever hopes he had for himself and Mary and their three kids, whatever hopes he had in this life's pilgrimage, were smashed to smithereens around his feet. The door to the future slammed shut in his face. He could see no way forward.

To be sure, he was shouting his guilt and his anger. Most especially, early that morning, he was shouting his terror to the high heavens.

Those two questions, "John, where are you heading? What kind of future are you building this morning?" opened the door to the future just enough of a crack that we could begin that four-hour conversation and develop that five-year relationship.

Don't get too caught up in the gun. By that time, having worked in a mission with alcoholics and their families, I had successfully gotten myself beaten up three times and seen my share of knives, handguns, and one shotgun. Bizarre events happen in the best of families. Especially when people are struggling with alcoholism. Now, to be sure, early that morning was the first time I had found myself standing in front of a semiautomatic submachine gun—and once in a lifetime is enough. But don't get too caught up in the gun.

Decisive events change our lives and shape our destinies. The most decisive event of that morning was my discovery of those two questions.

If I had asked the question I had been *taught* to ask in seminary, I would have said, "John, what's the problem?" There is considerable probability John might have spewed his problems all over the family room early that morning. Whether Mary or I or their three little kids or John—or any or all of us—would be here yet today is open to some considerable conjecture.

I don't know where those two questions came from, save God. They were not a part of my own perspective, my own way of thinking, my own frame of reference. They were not the way I had been looking at life. I would have said, "John, what's the problem?"

Valuing and Learning from Memory

One key, one possibility, for a whole, healthy life is hope. God invites us to a life of hope, not despair. There are discouragements, disheartenments, and defeats in life. We discover a life of hope by

- Valuing and learning from memory
- Seeing hope in the present and immediate future
- Seeing sources of hope in the distant future
- Having confidence there is hope in the next life

Hope is stronger than memory. Memory is strong. Hope is stronger.

Memory is strong. Memory influences our perceptions of the past, contributes to the shaping of our present understandings, and to the expectancies we have for our future. Memory is strong because we remember *tragic* events. These events marred and scarred our lives. These memories profoundly affect our sense of the future as well as the past.

We remember *sinful* events in which we participated. Some of these were simple, and some were dark and terrible. Some were events of commission and some of omission, where we failed to do that which we could have. The memory of all these sinful events is painful to us. We ask God's forgiveness and the forgiveness of others for our participation in those sinful events.

We remember *incidental* events. They were the little events and happenings that have somehow stuck with us. We don't know quite why we remember them, but they are present with us and shape our current perceptions and sense of the future.

We remember *celebrative* events. These joyful events, these happy times are balm for our souls. We share the birthdays, anniversaries, and events in which we celebrate accomplishments and achievements, good fun, good times. These memorable times enrich our lives.

Memory is strong because we remember *mentors* who loved us and helped us be who we are. To be sure, we remember many persons in our past. Some were family who loved us deeply. Some were dear friends. Some we simply knew. Some persons in our past harmed and injured us. And we most especially remember our mentors. They shared their wisdom and encouragement. They gave us the gift of their unconditional love. The memory of them affects our sense of the future as well as the past.

Most important, we remember *hope-fulfilled* events. We remember those events in which our deepest longings, yearnings, and hopes were decisively fulfilled.

Sometimes we make the mistake of assuming we are primarily creatures of custom, habit, and tradition. To be sure, we do develop a wide range of customs, habits, and traditions. But when we look closely at the traditions present in our lives, we discover the most powerful traditions are not about the past. The most powerful, profound traditions we recall are those events in which our own deepest yearnings, longings, and hopes for the future have been most dramatically and decisively fulfilled. These are not events solely of the past. These are events in which the future—the future of our hopes—has been decisively fulfilled.

One grouping of persons had some of their deepest longings, yearnings, and hopes decisively fulfilled in an event in 1945. Their deepest hopes for peace were realized. What they did in 1946, 1947, 1948, and every year since has strengthened the tradition of honoring that future-based, hope-fulfilled event.

Memory is strong, finally, because memory is about hope. It is in memory that we remember those decisive events of hope. That is what

Passover is about. That is what the Exodus is about. That is what Christmas is about. That is what Easter is about. That is what the open tomb and risen Lord and new life in Christ are about.

Value and learn from memory. Think through how memory lives itself out in your life. Think of the key memories that are decisive for you. Gather your compassion and wisdom, forgiveness and reconciliation. Come to peace with the tragic events. Accept God's forgiveness for the sinful events. Enjoy the simplicity of the incidental events. Savor the celebrative events. Gather your mentors around you. Rejoice in the hope-fulfilled events. Live in hope.

Seeing Hope in the Present and Immediate Future

Back in that early morning, four hours later, John still had the gun. From time to time, the gun wavered my way and Mary's, and the sense of sheer terror returned. It was now six o'clock. The sun was coming up. I could see we were making progress, and we were going to get beyond the mess of that time. But, we had gotten about as far as we were going to get for that morning. My curiosity got the better of me, and I asked, "John, where did you get the gun?"

He told me he had bought the gun earlier that year to protect his wife and his family.

I said, "John, you've spent the last four hours pointing the gun you bought to protect your wife and family at both your wife and your pastor." Although they were not members of our church, I am perfectly willing to claim to be someone's pastor when he needs the help of a pastor, and early that morning it looked to me like John needed all the help a pastor could give.

So I said, "John, you've spent the last four hours pointing the gun you bought to protect your wife and your family at both your wife and your pastor. Now, put it down, so we can get about the business of building the future."

And he did. And we did. Hope is stronger.

I am most grateful I did not, that morning, ask the question, "John, what's the problem?" Some people live life, regrettably, with what I call the four worst best questions. Some think they are among the best questions. If they are, they are among the worst of the best questions. These four questions are What are my problems? What are my needs? What are my concerns? and What are my weaknesses and shortcomings?

It is amazing how we are tempted to these questions. We draw up lengthy lists in our minds, and occasionally on paper, of our problems, needs, concerns, weaknesses, and shortcomings.

When we do this, we create for ourselves a harvest of despair, depression, and despondency. We think of all of our problems, our needs and concerns, our weaknesses and shortcomings. We are overcome. We have difficulty seeing a constructive future. We surround ourselves with the imagined enormousness of all our problems. We see no way forward.

It is as though we are drawn to these four worst questions as moths to a flame. Occasionally, loved ones and friends, sometimes with their own fair share of despair, and with alleged, well-meaning good intentions, press these questions upon us. They have their fair share of despair, but now that we feel our fair share of despair, they don't feel quite as bad because we now feel a whole lot worse. Misery does love company.

I call these four worst questions the four horsemen of the apocalypse. I call these questions the four assassins of hope. When we become preoccupied with these questions, we become distracted from our strengths. We are in the worst possible position to grow the strengths we really have.

I am not inviting us to ignore or deny the problems, needs, concerns, weaknesses, or shortcomings we have. But when you begin with your weaknesses and shortcomings, you are in the weakest position to do something about them. Start with your strengths. Claim your strengths. Build on your strengths. Now, you are in the strongest position to tackle your weaknesses and shortcomings. Now, you are in a position to create hope.

Look for hope. You will find it.

The gift of that morning with Mary and John was the discovery of those two invitational questions. In the time that has come and gone since that morning, I have discovered two more. These four invitational questions are central to our life's pilgrimage. I call them invitational questions because they are banner questions, to be held ever before us. They are not to be answered with precision and detail on the front end. They lead us forward. They help us to discover sources of hope in the present and immediate future:

Where are we headed?

What kind of future are we building?

What are our strengths, gifts, and competencies?

Who is God inviting us to serve in mission?

The question "Where are we headed?" confirms we can head toward the future God is promising and preparing for us. The most decisive understanding of God in the Old Testament is of the God who goes before the people, as a cloud by day and a pillar of fire by night, leading them toward the future He has promised and prepared. The most decisive understanding of God in the New Testament is the open tomb, the risen Lord, and new life in Christ. We are the people of the future. We are the Easter people. We are the people of hope.

We can study the past to discover how God has related with us, led us, and invited us forward. This is most beneficial. God was in the past, and at the same time has not stayed in the past. God acted graciously, mercifully, mightily, powerfully in the past and moved on to the present and the future. The person who looks to the present and the future sees God. That is where God now is. The question "Where are we headed?" confirms there is a future toward which we can head.

To be sure, the question, "Where have we been?" is a helpful question. The question "Where are we headed?" is a more helpful question. We can do certain things about where we have been. We can ask God's and other persons' forgiveness for our sins of omission and commission of the past. We can forgive others and ourselves. We can celebrate and give thanks to God and other persons for the accomplishments and achievements of the past. We can learn from our past. But we cannot change what has been. What has been has been. What we can do something with is where we are headed.

The question "What kind of future are we building?" confirms there is a future to build. We have this confidence: that amidst all the travails, troublements, tragedies of this life, God invites us to build a strong, solid future for our families and friends, our community and our world.

We are not born simply to cast about until we die. We are not here to simply live it up until our last breath. We are not here to live in rage and resignation about our death. We are not here to live in bitter resentment until the hour of our life passes and is no more.

We are here to build a healthy, constructive future for humankind, not solely for our families and friends alone but for our community and our world as well. We are here to help one another. We are here not to lament and complain, bemoan and whine, rage and resent, grab and get. We are here to serve and help, grow and develop, advance and improve.

God invites us to build a solid future for the world. The text in John 3:16 is very clear: "For God so loved the world . . ." We're invited to build a future richly, fully, for our families, our friends, our communities, our world. We are here to leave this world better off for our having been here.

The question "What are my strengths, gifts, and competencies?" confirms you have strengths and competencies with which to advance a whole, healthy life. There is no turning back. You are a person blessed with strengths. God has given you gifts and competencies with which to grow and build.

The question "Who is God inviting me to serve in mission?" suggests that your life has enduring, worthwhile value in the universe. Your life counts in lasting ways for God's mission. You can have the confidence, the assurance that who you are and what you share will serve God's mission richly and fully. In so doing, you will see hope in the present and immediate future of your life.

Seeing Hope in the Distant Future

We look for hope in the present and immediate future. We look for sources of hope in the distant future. When we cannot see sources of hope in the immediate future, we look for hope in the distant future. People live on hope, not on memory. Take away people's memories, and they become anxious. Take away people's hopes, and they become terrified. People live beyond the past. They live through change. They wrestle with conflict. The abiding, strongest dynamic is hope.

Martin Luther once said, "Everything that is done in the world is done by hope."

People long for and look for some sense of hope, some understanding of a future that is stable and reliable, not fleeting and fragile. We know there is much uncertainty in life. Philosophers of old tell us that everything changes, that the only certainty is change itself. Life does sometimes feel like that, and life is more than that. Finally, there are no live cynics; when one becomes a cynic, one is dead. We live in hope. Without hope, we are dead. With hope, we live.

The story is told of a fellow who was interested in learning how to parachute jump. He was in a hurry to learn. All of us are in a hurry at some point in our lives about something. He was sufficiently in a hurry that he rushed to a nearby airport and convinced the instructor that she could teach him everything he needed to know as they climbed into the plane and headed to twenty thousand feet.

By the time they got to twenty thousand feet, about all the instructor had time to do was get the parachute on him and discuss with him the basic principles of aerodynamics. Before the instructor could say yet another word, much to her surprise and shock, the fellow stepped to the open door of the plane, hollered "Geronimo!" and jumped.

Now, free-falling in midair, it dawns on him that he desperately needs the one key piece of data he failed to get from the instructor, namely, how do you open the bloomin' parachute?

As he plummets down to earth, he desperately yanks, jerks, grabs, pulls, hoping somehow he can get the parachute open. As he plummets down, he passes another fellow who is heading up. It catches him by surprise. Up there, you don't see too many people heading up.

He hollers over, "Helloooooooo, you know anything about opening a parachute?"

The man hollers back, "Noooooooo, you know anything about fixing a gas heater?"

Now, life sometimes does feel like plummeting-downs or blowing-ups. There seems to be one disaster and tragedy after another. God sees us through those times. God invites us to a life that looks less like plummeting down and blowing up. We are invited to a life that looks more hopeful, that leads us to the future God is promising and preparing for us.

God gives us the present. God gives us the future.

We have this certainty. We have this assurance. We have this confidence. The certainty is that God is with us, God loves us, God leads us forward, and God gives us the gift of hope. Prayer and worship, sacrament and spiritual life are resources with which we discover hope for our lives. The twelve keys, the twelve possibilities, help us develop strengths for our lives that advance our sense of hope, and the health and wholeness of our lives.

These twelve keys help us advance our lives in ways that are realistic and achievable. We will not succumb to a melancholy wishfulness. These twelve keys help to head toward objectives that are specific and concrete. We will not allow ourselves to become again the victim of the god of vague generalities. These twelve keys help us have solid time horizons; we will pace our future forward, and not try too much too soon. We will live in hope, one day at a time.

We live with some confidence and assurance that the future is promising. This does not mean that things are always getting better and better. It has more to do with the sense that, given the vicissitudes and difficulties, twists and turns, tragedies and trauma of life, God leads, sustains, and comforts us as we move forward. Some people, with diminished or no hope, have the sense their future is in their past. People who live in hope have the sense their past is in their future. Finally, our hope is in God. We live in the hope that God is leading us toward a promising future in the time to come.

Having Confidence There Is Hope in the Next Life

When we cannot see sources of hope in this life, we look for hope in the future of the next life. People postpone their hopes down the road. If they cannot see some fulfillment of their hopes in the present, immediate, or distant future, they long for some of their deepest hopes, yearnings, and longings to be fulfilled in the next life. Even when we see the fulfillment of some of our hopes in this life, we look toward sources of hope for the next-life future.

A sociologist once did a study in Appalachia. He concluded that the original pioneers, who cut down trees and built log cabins in those early years, had moved into Appalachia with a confident vision of hope. They saw themselves engaged in the building of a new and promised land.

But the sociologist concluded that those persons who now live in Appalachia eke out a bare, meager existence, clinging and clutching desperately to life, and no longer share their ancestors' sense of confident hope in the building of a new, promised land. The one place the sociologist failed to go was to those white-frame, clapboard churches up on the ridges and down in the hollows on Sunday morning. He did not hear the hymns sung there: "We Shall Gather at the River"; "In the Sweet By-and-By"; "Dwelling in Beulah Land."

People live on hope, more than memory.

At Piney Grove church on a Sunday morning, Mrs. Lott and I were standing out on the front porch of the church. Most of the people had gone, and it hadn't taken that long because there weren't that many people to go. She said to me, "Dr. Callahan, what I hope is that you will help us find a preacher this coming year who will share with us spiritual food."

What she was saying was this. Her husband had retired from the farm and was sort of rattling around the farmhouse with little to do. Her mother was ill of cancer, dying in a nearby nursing home. There were now strange, new kinds of people living up and down the road on which she had lived all her life. They dressed differently. Stayed up past ten o'clock at night.

She was saying that the hopeful ways in which she had made sense of life for the past twenty to twenty-five years were no longer working for her. She wanted a pastor who would help her make some sense out of everyday life, who would help her discover new sources of hope that would work for her in the present and immediate future, not simply the next-life future.

Nostalgia is not a retreat to the past. It is looking back to a time when some of our deepest hopes and longings were fulfilled. We draw that picture forward as the only picture of the future to which we can cling. We cling to it because no clearer picture seems available to us. We are all wise enough to know that "Grover's Corners" is no more. To be sure, it may exist now here, now there, in some hidden valley, not yet discovered in these last, twilight years of the twentieth century. But the "Our Towns" of our planet, like the town in Thornton Wilder's play, are no more.

There, everybody went to bed at ten o'clock at night. The train went through about the same time every night. There, Emily and George grew up, living side by side. They became good friends, fell in love, married. Life was settled and simple. But even in Grover's Corners, Emily died in childbirth. Grover's Corners is no more.

At New Liberty Church, when the kids rode their horses across the church cemetery, people got upset, not simply because they thought the horses and the kids were desecrating the ancestors of the past but because the horses and the kids were trampling on the church's symbol of the future. That church cemetery is not primarily a symbol of the past. The people know that those who are buried there are not really there.

They want to be buried there, not so they can lie beside so and so but because that cemetery is the symbol of each family's entrance into the kingdom of hope beyond this life. To be sure, the cemetery honors those who have gone before. But most important, the focus is on where they have gone: to a new and promised land, to the land of hope. People want to be buried there, because that cemetery is equally and fully the symbol of the future. They only fix the cemetery up once a year, just before homecoming.

Many, many churches across our country have a homecoming each year. These are not events that look to the past only. Church homecomings are events that look to the future. The homecoming is a present day, looking forward, proleptic event that looks to that great homecoming "beyond the river" when we will all be gathered as God's family.

Some make the mistake of thinking their task is to drag people reluctantly from the customs, habits, and traditions of the past into present. They work hard to get people to give up their past. They miss the fact that many people are not living in the past. They are living in the next-life future. Many have postponed their hopes to the next life. They can see no way in which even some of their hopes will be fulfilled in the present, immediate, or even distant future. So, they are living in the next-life future.

Sometimes we are the river people. We postpone our hope to the next life beyond the river.

Sometimes we are the flimsies people. We see no hope beyond the river; so we grasp for the fleeting flimsies of this life, the new car, the new job, the new house. We look for sources of hope among the things of this life. Even as we do, we know that they are shadows of hope. They do not last.

Sometimes we are the cliff people. We are frozen on the face of a cliff. Think about mountain climbing. Think about what it is like to find oneself on the face of a cliff where one can see no handholds and footholds ahead. We can see no way back to the handholds and footholds behind. What do we do in that predicament? We do one thing extraordinarily well. We freeze to the face of the cliff, clinging and clutching for dear life, fixed and immobile. We want no change. Because the only change we can see is the chasm and abyss below.

You and I, nearly frozen to the face of the cliff, would not want very much change either. Particularly when some cheery person comes along at the top of the cliff and hollers down in a loud voice, "Oh, it's easy! Just do as I tell you." We know what happens next. The person frozen to the face of the cliff is disrupted, alarmed, frightened even more. The person either clutches more fiercely or loses the handholds and falls into the abyss below.

What one does is join the person on the face of the cliff and gently and quietly coach them forward. Let's try the left hand. Three inches up. Here is this handhold. Now, the left foot. Two inches. Here is this foothold. Now here is another handhold. Now here is this foothold. Gently, quietly, inch by inch, you coach the person forward to new handholds and footholds.

When we find ourselves nearly frozen on the face of a cliff, we gently and quietly coach ourselves forward. We discover some person or group who helps us to new handholds and new footholds, to new sources of hope. Sometimes, we cling to this brief frailty we call life; we cling and clutch so hard that we miss the thrill and joy of simply being alive. We are so concerned about losing life, that we never really find it.

Sometimes you and I are the river people. Sometimes, we are the flimsies people. Sometimes, we are the cliff people. When we live life at our best, we are the Easter people. We know our hope is in God. We serve, not to earn our future but in humble gratitude that our future has already been given to us. We live with the confidence, the assurance that the sources of hope are not in our own doings, graspings, and clutchings. We live, knowing that we are the Easter people, the people of the open tomb, the risen Lord, with new life in Christ. We live in hope.

The kingdom of God is now here, now there. The kingdom happens in every event of mission and serving, in every event of compassion, in every event of reconciliation, wholeness, caring, and justice, in every event of hope. There, the kingdom happens.

At the same time, the kingdom is not yet—in its fullness. Some people share only half of the good news. They speak only of the this-worldly kingdom. Others focus only on an otherworldly, next-life understanding of the kingdom. The truth of the kingdom is twofold. The kingdom has come. The kingdom is coming. The reality is the kingdom has happened. The reality is its fulfillment is before us.

There is direct correlation between living and hope, between a whole, healthy life and a confident sense of hope. The two go hand in hand. One cannot do one without the other. It is in living a life strongly influenced by hope that a life of serving is developed. Hope enriches living. Living enriches hope. We live forward or downward to our hopes.

In Proverbs 23:18, we discover these words: "Surely there is a future, and your hope will not be cut off." In Romans 8:6, we find, "To set the mind on the flesh [preserving one's life] is death, but to set the mind on the Spirit [serving in mission, with compassion and hope] is life and peace."

By grace we are alive, and this is not our own doing; it is the gift of God. Our life is the gift of God. By grace our mission is not our own doing; it is the gift of God. By grace we share compassion, and this is not our own doing; it is the gift of God. By grace our hope is not in ourselves or in our own doing. Our hope is the gift of God. Live in hope.

o
_____

Almighty and Enduring God,
    Let us live this life with compassion and hope.
    Let us love, richly and fully, the persons with whom we share
this life.
        Let us live a life of confidence and assurance in Your grace.
    Let us hope for more beyond the grave.
        Receive us into the life to come.
        Amen.

6

COMMUNITY

I INVITE YOU to be kind with Eunice.

Late that Saturday morning, Mrs. Perkins called. There was distress and concern in her voice. She said, "Ken, come quick. Something has happened with Eunice."

Mrs. Perkins (in my mind, because of her gentle, kind nature, she was always "Mrs. Perkins") had never called me in that urgent way before. I had my own concerns for her sister, Eunice. I went quickly. When I got to Mrs. Perkins's home, she was outside on the porch, anxious, troubled, pacing up and down. She ran to greet me, throwing her arms around me, "Oh, Ken, something has happened with Eunice. I don't know what to do."

That spring, Mrs. Perkins and I had stood day by day at Tom's hospital bedside. He was gravely ill, lingered long, and finally died. I shared the funeral service with Mrs. Perkins and some of her friends. Three days later, Mrs. Perkins and I went out to the cemetery and stood by Tom's grave and had prayers with one another, with Tom, and with God.

It was a tough time for Mrs. Perkins. She and Tom had met in grade school, grown up together, become good friends, married, and lived a long, wonderful, close life together. They were good partners. He was gone. It was a tough time for her.

Eunice was Mrs. Perkins's maiden sister, born on the old homestead in Nearly Nowhere, in a neighboring state. She had grown up in the old homestead and lived her whole life there.

On the occasion of Tom's death, she did what good sisters do. She gathered up all her courage and left the world she knew and came to the big city to spend a few weeks with her good sister so Mrs. Perkins would not be by herself during the day. She would have company at each meal. She would not feel alone as she passed Tom's favorite chair and, in her mind,

still saw him sitting there. And, of an evening when Mrs. Perkins went to
bed, she would know there was someone in the house with her.

Mrs. Perkins and Eunice had come to church. I had been by the home
several times. Eunice and I had become friends.

In July, Eunice was still there. She lingered longer than she planned. It
was a hard time for her sister. Toward the end of July, I began to have my
own concerns about Eunice. You could almost see a tightness appear on
her face, a look of scared panic began to creep into her eyes.

So that Saturday morning in early August when the phone call came, I
went quickly.

Mrs. Perkins explained she had been in the kitchen early that morning
fixing breakfast. Eunice was coming and leaving, coming and leaving,
coming and leaving the kitchen. She simply assumed that Eunice was
doing some things around the house, helping with the chores.

When Mrs. Perkins had breakfast ready, she called Eunice. Eunice did
not come. She called again. Eunice still did not come. She went hunting
for Eunice. She could not find her. Having looked all through the house,
she finally found her in the bathroom.

This is where I invite you to be kind with Eunice.

For whatever reason, early that morning, Eunice felt led to know this
was the day to wash clothes. For whatever reason, she was drawn to
washing the clothes—it would be the best place, she thought—in the bathtub, not in the washing machine.

Eunice gathered up all the clothes she could find and put them in the
bathtub, turned the water on, and put in soap. In her coming and leaving the kitchen, Eunice went into the pantry and gathered whatever
strange array of condiments she could find on the shelves and brought
them and dumped them into the bathtub. Corn syrup, cereal, pickles,
jam, olives—just whatever was on the shelves—she came in, picked up
the foodstuffs, opened them, and dumped them into that ungodly mess
in the bathtub.

When Mrs. Perkins found her beloved sister, Eunice was stirring the
ungodly mess with the upside-down handle of a broom. Mrs. Perkins was
understandably upset. They were mostly her clothes in that mess. Eunice
hadn't brought that many clothes with her.

Mrs. Perkins naturally objected to what her good sister, Eunice, was
doing. Mrs. Perkins almost held the words in check, but they just came
tumbling out. The two of them exchanged a mixture of hurried, angry
words. This reminded Eunice she had forgotten the pillowcases and the
bedsheets. She went and got them off the beds and dumped those in the
ungodly mess as well.

Even two sisters who dearly love one another, who are simply trying to help one another through this life's pilgrimage as best they can, have been known to exchange words and gently tussle, shove, and push in a hallway on a Saturday morning.

All the stresses and strains of Tom's death and Eunice's weeks in that strange, big city had been too much. With the sharp exchange of words, and the tussling and pushing, Eunice went to the kitchen to find the largest butcher knife she could lay her hands so she could hold her sister at bay, while she did what she felt she had been called to do. Seeing the large butcher knife pointed her way, Mrs. Perkins went to the phone and called me.

In the brief time it took me to get there, some further words were exchanged, more heated this time. The result was that Eunice did in two sets of curtains with the butcher knife and was working on the sofa in the living room. That was why Mrs. Perkins was standing outside on the porch.

It's amazing what kind of help you cannot get, even living in a big city, on a Saturday morning. We called the police department, and they said they would come just as soon as she stabbed one of us. She hadn't done anything—yet. Well, Mrs. Perkins and I drew a line in the sand, and we both stood on one side and we talked it over and wondered who would step across the line and volunteer to be the one to be stabbed. Neither of us stepped across the line.

We called the county mental health association. We got a pleasant, cheerful voice on the telephone. It was an answering machine, informing us that the offices would be open at 9:00 A.M. on Monday and to please call back then. Right then, on Saturday, Monday morning at nine o'clock looked like a long time away.

We called the nearby hospital. Could they help? "Sure," they said, "bring her over." The "bringing her over" part was a stumbling block. That did not look like something we were going to be able to do right then.

We did what good family do. We called the brother and the nephew in Nearly Nowhere, and held the fort for three long, long, long hours, as they drove down in their car. A better way to say it would be "as they flew down in their car." It's a four-hour trip for anyone driving really fast. They did it in three hours. It's amazing what family do when someone in the clan is in trouble.

When they got there, we did what good family do. We stood around in the front yard, the brother, the nephew, Mrs. Perkins, and I, talking, wondering what we could do now. Finally, we came upon the idea that maybe Eunice would do better at home.

"Let's take Eunice home."

When that idea found common agreement, the brother and the nephew said, "Would you go with us?" I said, "I don't see how I could. It's now late Saturday afternoon, and we have three worship services on Sunday morning, 8:00, 9:30, and 11:00. I don't see how I could hardly get back for the 8:00 o'clock service."

The brother said, "Oh, don't worry. There is a mail plane at 2:00 A.M. out of the nearby airport. We'll see you are on that plane."

It was amazing to me, when I said yes I would go with them, how quickly they both jumped into the front seats of the car, saying, "I'm sure you prefer to ride in the back seat with Eunice."

I said to Eunice, "Eunice, we're heading home. Give your sister a hug and a kiss. It's been a good visit. You have helped greatly. We're heading home. Lay the butcher knife here on the porch. We'll leave it behind. It belongs to your sister. Give her a hug and a kiss."

She did.

I helped Eunice into the car, closed the door, and walked, with fear and trembling, around the back of the car to get in on my side. I had not even gotten the door closed before we were heading out of the drive to the old homestead in Nearly Nowhere.

We did take four hours on the trip back. It was four long, long, long, long hours in the back seat of the car on the way to Nearly Nowhere, with Eunice. There was upsetness and anger, tears and sorrow. There was sullen silence. Words of recrimination and words of regret. There was quiet talk. Some laughter.

Eunice taught me an extraordinary lesson that day. You could almost see it as we got near familiar places and faces. You could almost see the tightness relax from her face. As we turned down the dirt road—more dirt than road—leading to the old homestead, you could almost see the look of panic recede from her eyes. We pulled up in the front yard—more dirt than yard—of the old homestead. I went around, opened the door, and helped Eunice out. As best one can be, Eunice was virtually herself again.

A Sense of Roots

One key, one possibility, for a whole, healthy life is community. God invites us to a life of community, not loneliness. We are at our best when, amidst difficult times, we have community. Our best instincts lead us to community. We innately know we are not created for isolation, solitariness. We may, from time to time, feel a sense of being forsaken. We feel alone. Even then, we know we are meant to live in community. We search for roots, place, belonging, family, and friends. Sometimes our search is desperate, profound.

People teach me that they define community in a wide range of ways. For some people, community means one thing. For others, it means something else. What helps you live a whole, healthy life is to discern how a sense of community enriches you and to nurture that strength forward as you develop

- A sense of roots
- A sense of place
- A sense of belonging
- A sense of family and friends

The closer we are to home, the more like our best true selves we become. The clinical terms for Eunice's dilemma that Saturday morning are psychological disorientation and societal dislocation. The massive city had crushed in upon Eunice. The bigness and business of the city contributed to her societal dislocation. She knew how to live in the old homestead, but the pace, speed, crowdedness, confusion of the big city became more than she could handle.

The loss of roots, place, and belonging, the hardly knowing anyone, the bewilderment, the bafflement of the city contributed to her psychological disorientation. She could not quite figure out who she was or where she was anymore. That morning, Eunice was shouting out that it was more than she could take. She needed to be home.

We all have our fair share of psychological disorientation and societal dislocation. In our time, the pace is fast, furious. The city and even the countryside are teeming. Stress is high. We see our fair share of bizarre events, even in the best of families. People act out their desperate plea to find home, to discover roots, beginnings. People search for their family tree as a way of discovering their roots, to discover from whom they came.

A sense of roots contributes to our sense of community. In earlier times, people would sometimes ask, "Who are your kin?" The question was asked as a way of discovering some sense of a person's roots. In effect, the question was, "Who are your roots?" The sense of clan, of kinfolk, of lineage is an important source of community.

Emma was abandoned by her father. So she thought. In the middle years of her life, she learned that her mother had left her father. This insight was to come later; growing up, she had the sense of being rejected. She thought of herself as unworthy. It was somehow her fault that she had been abandoned by her father.

She developed a deep fear of being abandoned in many of her relationships. She sometimes became overly possessive in order, so she felt, to
avoid being abandoned. She would press her girlfriends too much to
spend all of their time with her. When she began to date, she would too
quickly press her new boyfriend into going steady, into spending virtually
every waking moment with her. All of this was to reassure herself that she
would never again be abandoned.

What began to help her, in her early twenties, was to discover a richer
sense of her roots, of the larger family from whom she had come. The
August before her senior year at the university she made a trip to see her
great aunt, her mother's mother's sister. She had not seen her for years.
Driving down the road to her great aunt's home, she couldn't quite
remember how long ago it had been. She had a dim memory of her great
aunt visiting her shortly after she had been told her father "had gone
away." She must have been three or four years old. She could remember
the living room. She could vaguely see the faces of her mother and grandmother. She could remember the nervousness and tenseness that had been
in the air. A great void, a deep emptiness, had come into her life that day.
It seemed so long ago.

As she was visiting with her great aunt, they had tea on the side porch;
her great aunt brought out the family album. They pored over the album
for the whole of that warm, pleasant afternoon. There were pictures of
aunts and uncles, great aunts and great uncles, grandmothers and grandfathers, great grandmothers and great grandfathers, and cousins upon
cousins. There were pictures of family reunions on the old farm, of wed-
dings in churches and homes, of funerals in graveyards, of graduations
and new babies. Her great aunt was the family historian. She had a wealth
of knowledge about the kin and clan.

That afternoon, Emma began coming to peace with her feelings of having been abandoned. With the love and insight of her great aunt, she was
able to discover the larger family of whom she was a part. She began to
discover her roots and her more extensive family. As a consequence, she
was able to develop a richer sense of community in her life.

In a larger sense, the quest of anthropology, archaeology, paleontology,
and the like is humanity's search for its roots, for its beginnings. There is
the hope that, with some understanding of our roots, of from whom and
from whence we have come, we will have deeper insight into who we are,
the journey we have traveled, and hopefully therefore some clues as to
where we are headed. As we discover some sense of our roots, we begin
to build a sense of community in our lives.

A Sense of Place

A sense of place contributes to our sense of community. For some people, their sense of place has regional ties. Dan has traveled his sales territory for years, covering five states. He knows it like the back of his hand. It is the setting in which he has lived his whole work life. For some, their sense of place is broad, vast, far-ranging. Sally, over time, has lived in virtually every section of our country. As a consequence, for her, the whole country is the setting for her many homes. Some people have a regional, nomadic sense of place.

For some persons, the sense of place remains singularly immediate, usually with a specific address or locale in mind. It may be an apartment, a trailer, a tenement, or a house. It may be a specific neighborhood or a specific community.

My wife Julie's memories of growing up are of living the whole time in the same two-story house on Seventeenth Street in Cuyahoga Falls, Ohio. She lived her first year of life on Seventeenth. Then, for nearly three years, her family lived in neighboring Stow. She has some dim memories of the house in Stow. They moved back to the house on Seventeenth when she was around four years old, where she lived for fourteen more years.

The house had a summer porch on the right-hand side. It was a pleasant place to spend a cool summer evening, watching the lightning bugs through the screen of the porch. The driveway to the detached one-car garage was to the left of the house. There was a side door to the house just by the driveway. It really served as the main door. You would go into the landing, go up three steps, and be in the kitchen. There were two great old trees in the front yard, and richly yielding plum, apple, pear, and cherry trees in the back. There was a clothes chute from the second floor of the house to the basement. She and Doris Jean, her cousin, would have great fun sending messages to one another up and down the clothes chute on a string.

Some time back, Julie and I made a trip to Cuyahoga Falls for her high school class reunion. We drove around the town, like so many of us do, taking pictures of all the houses in which we had lived, remembering the times we lived in each. We took pictures of her home on Seventeenth Street and of all the places where I had lived.

In my growing up years, I lived in numerous houses. In addition to his regular job, my dad, to help our family advance, would build a house, we would move in, finish it out, sell it for some profit, and do the same thing again elsewhere. Sometimes, he would buy an existing house, fix it up, sell it, and move on. All of these moves happened within the same town, Cuyahoga Falls.

There was the bungalow on Jennings and the two-story house on Wadsworth. There was the triplex across the river on Myrtle, where my three cousins and our grandmother lived on the second floor and my mother, brother, and I lived on the first floor. My dad and my uncle were away at the war.

Then there was the duplex on Third near Crawford Elementary School, the spacious house on Eleventh with the flower gardens in the back yard, the larger home we built on Jefferson and Thirteenth, with the vegetable garden across the whole of the backyard. My newspaper route covered the one hundred and some homes in the area. There was the house with the breezeway on Eleventh and the three-story home on State Road. I have some sense of place for each of these houses in which I lived.

For our family, Sunday dinner was an important part of those times on the move. For many years we would go for Sunday dinner after church to my grandparents' home on the small knoll at the top of Brace Place. There would be good food and great fun. During the course of the week, I would frequently visit with them. My grandmother could make the best oatmeal cookies. She freely gave her recipe to many people. Hers seemed always to turn out best. We would pick cherries from their tree out back, me standing on the ladder with a basket. Later, a warm, sweet cherry pie would appear on the kitchen table. My grandfather could fix anything. He was quiet, unassuming. There were good times on Brace Place.

So, for me, when I think of place, in my growing up years, I think of the whole of Cuyahoga Falls because I lived all over the town. Especially, I think of those warm, happy times at my grandparents' home on Brace Place. Julie has a primary sense of place in her early years with the one house on Seventeenth Street. For both of us, our sense of place is the special place where we live now and the continuum of places we have lived together since our marriage.

Some of us have learned a broad, regional, wide-ranging, nomadic sense of place. Some of us have learned a singular, local, immediate, settler sense of place. Our experiences in life have helped us to learn whatever sense of place we now have. In reality, we all have the capacity to learn both a regional, nomadic and a local, more settled sense of place. There is both nomad and settler within us. Some of us have learned one of these more fully. Some have developed the other. Both possibilities are with us. We can learn and develop both.

In recent times, many people have developed excellent skills in living in a regional, nomadic fashion. They have learned how to live with rapid job transfers. They live two years here, and two years there. Because of the business in which they work, they have learned how to move every two to three years, and to develop in their lives a sense of place. Persons in the military, whether growing up in it or following it as a career, develop skills in moving. People who leave their originating place, go to college, and then quickly move through their first, second, third, and so on job placements develop excellent competencies in a nomadic way of living.

In earlier times, the massive migrations across the planet were more of an extended family clan nature. The whole clan gathered itself up and moved to a new setting. They did this with some frequency, following the seasons, the water, and the herds. In our time, nomadic movements are more individual and singular. One person, or part of the family clan, may move, now here, now there. They learn to live in a moving, transitory way. Their sense of place is regional and nomadic.

We also find a sense of place as we look to some long-lost house that was comforting, familiar, warm, and cozy. It may be the place of pleasant memories while growing up, or the place where we took our family vacations, or the place where we mostly raised our kids. It may not be where we are now. Anyone who has lived in twenty-three-plus places tends to think of one, two, or three as distinctively home. Most importantly, we tend to search for some place in the present that conveys the spirit of home.

In our time, the sense of place is becoming both more regional and more local, both more nomadic and more settled. We are developing an even larger regional sense of place with the discoveries of the immensity of the stars and solar systems in which we live. Our sense of place is taking on an intergalactic, light-years dimension. The immensity of the universe teaches us the immensity of the home God gives us. We are increasingly aware that our sense of place is in the stars. With the interconnections of trade and commerce, cultures and peoples, we are developing a larger regional sense of mutual reciprocity and interdependence with one another across the planet.

At the same time, we are developing an even more local sense of place. Contributing to this is the speed of transportation and the diversity of communications systems that have evolved, and are evolving at an even more rapid rate. The trips that used to take weeks and months now happen in hours and days. The messages that used to take days and weeks to get there now get there in seconds and minutes. These networks of travel and communications continue to bring us closer together.

These two dynamics—a larger sense of regional and a closer sense of local—are revising the ways we think about place. Further, these two dynamics contribute to our search for a sense of place that is distinctively personal, specific, particular, and individual. As we discover some sense of place, helpful for our time, we deepen the sense of community in our lives.

A Sense of Belonging

A sense of belonging contributes to our sense of community. The search for community is the search for belonging, the search for people as well as roots and place. We need to belong. We long to belong. We want to have the sense of belonging.

The proliferation of groups, in recent times, illustrates how important, indeed, how desperate, the search for belonging is. The vast arrays of groups that have emerged are amazing to behold. There is virtually a group for every interest, however particular and singular that interest might be. In these groups, both in their rapid growth and their considerable diversity, we see evidence of how profoundly important having a sense of belonging is.

Some groups are formal, institutional, systematic, and well organized. They have a planned, established nature. They customarily have regular meetings or gatherings. There is usually some set of criteria for membership. Frequently, there are officers. There may even be written bylaws to inform the group's focus and direction. There is a kind of institutional sense to these groups. There is an orderly spirit to their life together.

Some groups are more informal, relational, relaxed, and spontaneous. Such groups are loosely developed and casual. They have a spontaneous, flexible nature. Their gatherings are occasional and impromptu, almost on the spur of the moment. There is an open spirit as to who is part of the grouping. The leadership of the group varies with the activity of the group. There are unwritten customs and values in the grouping to inform the group's focus and direction, but there are no written bylaws. There is a kind of relational sense to these groups. There is a common, shared spirit to their life together.

These more informal groupings are more like a collection of persons who relate with one another in a spirit of casualness and informality. In recent times, there has been a modest shift from the formal, institutional groups toward the informal, relational groupings. That is, people used to find their sense of belonging basically in the formal, organized groups in the culture. Increasingly, people are finding their sense of belonging in the informal, spontaneous groupings that abound in our time.

We enhance our sense of belonging as we participate in one or more groups, formal or informal. There is a wide diversity of groups in our time. Some possibilities include groups whose focus is

vocational, professional	arts, music
sociological, ethnic	educational
geographical, neighborhood	retired
human hurt, hope	political, governmental
life stage	recreational
civic, community	business
hobbies, interests	religious

The list goes on and on. I encourage you to develop a healthy mix of formal and informal groups; the mix helps you deepen your sense of belonging.

In order to have some sense of belonging, continuity, and consistency, each group, formal or informal, creates for itself these individuating qualities and traits:

o A set of goals and values important to the persons in the group or grouping

o A set of customs, habits, and traditions

o A communications network and language dialect

o A leadership and decision-making process

o A sacred place of meeting, sometimes multiple places

o A common shared vision of the future

These qualities give each group a sense of identity and help each person have a sense of belonging.

We frequently belong to more than one group. In an earlier time, on the remote frontier, the only group accessible was the homestead, family group. The advantage of the proliferation of groups in our time is the array of possibilities available to us. We have the ability to be part of several groups. At a given time in our lives, we may be part of an interest group such as quilting; a vocational, professional group; a music group; a recreational group; and a civic, community group.

One of these groups may become, for a specific time in our lives, a primary grouping. That is, we discover a primary sense of belonging in this group. We have the sense of being intimately part of the group. We derive much of our sense of belonging, for this time in our lives, from this specific group.

We are also part of other groups, some of which are

o Secondary groups, from which we derive an important, auxiliary sense of belonging

o Associational groups, which are part of our lives, and from which we derive some sense of belonging

o To a lesser extent, occasional groups, in which from time to time we participate and that we find helpful

Dan is part of a large extended family, which though scattered across the planet keeps in touch almost daily through phone calls, letters, cards, and e-mail. Within the town in which he lives, he and his wife share close primary relationships with a group of good friends. The people with whom he works provide an important sense of belonging. He is active in his church and participates in several local clubs and organizations, and from time to time he shares in golfing and fishing outings with a group of friends from his college days.

In a certain sense, we experience belonging at four levels: primary, secondary, associational, and occasional. Both formal groups and informal groups enrich our sense of belonging. Some of these are primary; some are secondary, associational, or occasional.

In the course of our lives, an occasional group may advance to become a primary group, while what was a significant primary group recedes into the background and becomes an occasional group. The key is the extent to which each group contributes to our sense of community. Through groups we discover a sense of belonging, helpful for where we are at this time in life, and we develop a rich, full sense of community.

The Sense of Family and Friends

A sense of family and friends contributes to our sense of community. The search for community is the search for family and friends, as well as the search for roots, place, and belonging. The phrase "home is where the heart is" confirms that home is more than place. A house does not finally make a home; people do. A house is a roof under which we store our stuff. A family is a grouping of people who share their hearts and lives with each other. A family is a grouping of persons who share informal, significant relationships of loving and living with one another.

Discovering this deeper sense of family, friends, and home is increasingly difficult in our time. The genealogical, extended family clans of an earlier frontier time used to deliver this everyday sense of family, but many of these family clans have been scattered asunder, across the landscape. Thus, we look for a deep, rich, full sense of family and friends wherever we can find it. That is, we look for some network of persons who are family and friends with us. Indeed, we actively participate in creating this informal grouping of persons who become our family.

This family group may include some of the persons who are part of our biological family, but it is no longer the case, given the dynamics of the culture, that one's everyday life family automatically includes all of one's biological family. Our everyday family group frequently includes persons from the formal and informal groups in which we participate. Our network of "family and friends" may include, for example, four people from one group, three from another group, one from another, two from another, and four who are not part of any group in which we participate. Our family group overlaps and transcends the biological family and the formal and informal groups in which we participate.

There is a dynamic to this informal, significant relational family network. There is a consistency: some persons, year after year, are family with us. There is a spontaneity: some persons are family with us for this time in our lives, and then they move on. There is a pattern to our life together. We develop some sense of customs, habits, and traditions with one another. There is a flexibility to our life together. We discover new ways to be family with one another.

For some of us, our everyday, informal family network includes three to five to eight persons. For some, our family includes fifteen to thirty or more persons. Whatever the size, and that varies from time to time, this family group is most helpful in our lives. The formal groups help with our sense of belonging. The informal groups help. Our family group helps greatly with our rich, full sense of community.

For some persons, their family group is primarily their work group. Many persons live in what I call a vocational village. In an earlier time, the originating, genealogical family clan and the vocational village—the farms and the craft guilds of that time—frequently overlapped. The clan group and the vocation group were virtually the same. In our time, this is less so. At the same time, for some people, their vocational group, with whom they invest much of their time and energy each day, has become virtually their "family" group.

Sometimes, it is the interest group, whether quilting or bowling, that becomes virtually the family group we gather around us. Most of us have learned how to discover and create this network of family and friends who have an ongoing, informal presence in our lives, precisely to fill the void left by the scattered nature of our genealogical, extended family clan.

Where the originating clan continues to function well in everyday family ways, people have not needed to learn how to develop their family network group. Wherever the originating grouping has been scattered, disrupted, or torn asunder by conflict, people create their own informal, significant relational family group to fulfill this sense of everyday community in their lives.

Our everyday family group helps us in these ways. First, simply and importantly, the group helps us share everyday life in supportive and loving ways. Second, the group gathers with us to share celebrations, birthdays, anniversaries, and general good times together. Third, in tragic times, when we are in need of care and shepherding, our informal family group puts its arms around us and walks with us through the valley of the shadow. In times of disappointment and difficulty, the group is there. Likewise, we are there with and for them in tragic times as well. Fourth, the group helps us be open and inclusive, warm and welcoming persons. Healthy groups are not closed and exclusive, clannish and cliquish.

The closer our sense of family, the more open we are. The more fragile and feeble the sense of family, the more closed a group is likely to be. When group members sense the fragility of their own relationships with one another, the group closes up as a self-protective measure. The more secure in its own relationships, the more open a group is. We are not meant for isolation and insulation. We benefit from being part of an open, inclusive group, encouraging our own best instincts toward warm, welcoming community.

We, in our time, have a profound search for community, for family, for friends. Be kind with Eunice. Sometimes we are all Eunice. We do not quite know who we are or where we are. We experience our own share of psychological disorientation and societal dislocation. Our search for community becomes most urgent, most desperate, most profound. We long for roots, place, belonging. We long for family and friends. When we find them—when we feel surrounded with that which is familiar in places and faces of good friends and family—we become our true selves again. As we discover some sense of family and friends, helpful for our time, we discover and experience a profound sense of community in our lives.

Deepen your sense of roots. Advance your sense of place. Develop your sense of belonging. Build your sense of family. You will have a rich, full sense of community in your life. In Ephesians 2:19 (NEB), we discover these words of assurance: "Thus you are no longer aliens in a foreign land, but fellow-citizens with God's People, members of God's household."

We gather as a new family, in the presence of God, and we find a sense of roots, place, belonging, family, and friends. We discover sharing and caring, reconciliation and wholeness, openness and community. With the amazing richness of this community, we become our best true selves. We become whole, healthy persons.

———— o ————

Loving and Holy God,
   when we are lonely, surround us with Your love.
      When we feel dislocated, help us to know Your presence.
      When we become disoriented, guide us in Your way.
Help us discover roots, place, and belonging.
   Help us cherish the friends You give us along life's way.
Grant us the gift of family, who love us for who we are,
   and whom we love for who they are.
Help us to find home, to be our best true selves.
   In the name of Christ, we pray. Amen.

7

LEADERSHIP

DOROTHY WOULD CALL EARLY. There were a whole series of Saturday mornings when she would call and say something like, "I'm in the bathroom. The razor blades are on the counter. I can't take it any more. I'm just calling to say good-bye."

Her phone call would cause me to talk her through it till sunrise, or, while Julie held the fort on the phone, I would rush over to help. These were not "wolf, wolf" phone calls. They were dead serious. She knew how to slash her wrists correctly to make it to the other side of the river, and she had nearly done it three times.

I finally figured out her fear: it was chaos. We are fearful of chaos. Her work, her job delivered her sufficient structure that she could make it through the week. But Friday at five o'clock she entered a world of chaos, a world of no structure. By early Saturday morning, with her fears, her anxieties, her terror of chaos, she was ready to call this world quits.

I began to phone her at work on Friday morning, at her ten o'clock break. She with a sheet of paper and a pencil, I with a sheet of paper and a pencil, together we would structure her weekend. Who she would see. Where. When. What she would do. We put together a detailed schedule that organized her time from five o'clock Friday until early Saturday morning. Then we put in place, in detail, the schedule for all of Saturday and Sunday as well.

It worked. Then it didn't. Then it did. It didn't. It did. It didn't. It did. It didn't. Then it did and did and did.

Some years went by. Dorothy called. She had been transferred several years before to another city. She was coming through town and hoped we could visit together over lunch. She wanted to thank me for all those times I had talked her through to sunrise, and for all those times I had rushed over. Most especially, she wanted to thank me for the ten-minute phone calls on Friday mornings.

She said to me, "I want you to know that it was in those Friday morning phone calls that I began to learn how to take control of my life. I learned how to lead my own life."

Being Proactive and Intentional

One key, one possibility, for a whole, healthy life is leading your own life. God invites us to *lead* our lives, not simply react to what life brings us. We are at our best when, amidst the chaos, the excesses, the loss of power, and the conflicts that abound, we develop the resources for leading our lives:

- Being proactive and intentional about how we live our lives
- Sharing a sense of balance with people around us
- Rediscovering a sense of power in our own lives
- Having the capacity to deal with conflict

With these qualities well in place, you will lead your life solidly and helpfully.

Leadership is, first of all, leadership of oneself. As you can see, I am not talking about leadership primarily as a function in an institution or organization, but as a way of living life. A rich, full understanding of leadership has more to do with how you live and lead your own life than how you lead an organization. How you lead yourself shapes how you lead others. Too be sure, leadership in institutions, organizations, and movements is important, but here we are focusing on how you advance and build a sense of leadership for your own life.

We are proactive, not reactive, about our own life. There are experiences of chaos; Dorothy knew those well. There are times when other people seek to control our lives. Some people always seek to control their children. Even after their children have grown up, married, and had children of their own, these people continue to manipulate and maneuver what their children do. There are occasions when we are uncertain as to which way to head in life. Alice, in Wonderland, could not decide which way to go, which road to take. We sometimes find ourselves in a similar dilemma. Uncertainty and doubt are part of life.

A helpful understanding of leading is this: to lead is to guide on a way. We are invited to have some sense of direction for our lives, to have some feeling of where we are headed, to have some sense of control in our lives. The old saying is, "I can control myself. I cannot control what other people do. I can control how I deal with other persons. I can control how I allow others to affect me."

We are invited not simply to live our lives. We are invited to lead our lives. Indeed, we are the best persons to lead our lives. We are invited to exercise leadership in our own lives.

Three men came, silently and swiftly, from nowhere, and robbed and raped Sandra and her two friends. Afterwards, their sense of devastation, their sense of being victims, was enormous. Sandra told her family, "I am not going to be overcome by what they have done. I am not going to allow what they have done to control me. I am a survivor. I will get beyond this. I will lead my life." Like the survivors of calamities and tragedies of current times and of events of desolation and despair in times gone by (the survivors of the Holocaust come to mind), Sandra has survived. She has gone on to lead a healthy, productive life.

Her family and friends took heart from her example. In effect, they said, "We are not going to allow ourselves to be overcome by what those three men did to her. If Sandra is not overcome by this, we will not be overcome either. If she can lead her life forward, we will too. We are not going to do any less than she is."

The courage and compassion, the sense of presence, and the capacity to survive that Sandra demonstrated gave those around her the ability to move forward as well. We either lead our lives amidst the events that happen, or we allow those events to control us.

Molly's operation lasted four hours longer than planned. In the hospital waiting room, her family became more and more anxious as each long hour slipped silently by. The surgery was to last six hours. Finally, after the tenth hour had come and gone, it was over. Somehow, Molly survived the operation. The doctors said they thought they had gotten all of the cancer out. Weeks of radiation followed. The treatments were just to be certain, as best one can be in such precarious circumstances.

Through it all, Molly did well. There were fearful, panicky moments. There were doubts and despair. There were times of anxious laughter and quiet tears. There was in Molly the sense that, as best she could, she would survive, that she would not allow the events that were happening to her to diminish her sense of worth and her sense of direction for her life. She was not going to allow herself to become a victim. She did know she was going to lead her life one day at a time, as best she could.

As best we can, amidst the events life brings to us, we exercise control over our lives. With the grace of God, we lead wise, caring lives. We are not blown now hither, now yon. We are not the victims of every tragedy and trauma, every whim and sadness, every fad and foolishness. With wisdom and anticipation we have some promising sense of purpose and future for our lives. We encourage and support, reinforce and strengthen those around us. We help others as we give leadership in our own lives.

Leading one's life, being proactive in one's life, does not mean being a front-and-center, high-challenge, take-charge, deeply committed, charge-ahead-on-all-fronts kind of person. That picture of being a leader is, in fact, less helpful. That way of leading is really better understood as a way of pushing and shoving, demanding and oppressing, wanting one's own way. It is not really leading.

We lead our lives in a person-centered, people-centered, relational way. We do not become wrapped up in rules and regulations, policies and procedures. We are not preoccupied with position, authority, and power. We are not caught up in an endless merry-go-round of processes. We do not try to charm our way forward with soothing sayings. We do not threaten those around us with one troubling crisis after another.

The simple, wise thing we do is to lead in our own lives. We are not so preoccupied about leading others. We are focused on leading ourselves. We have come to understand that learning how to lead ourselves in this life is more helpful than being concerned about leading others. Leadership has more to do with us. The person who has learned how to lead herself can lead others. The person who has not learned how to lead in his own life has difficulty leading others in their lives.

In our leading of our lives, we are interested in building a whole, healthy life and in helping other people build their lives. We seek to discover new communities of mission and service amidst the intense, increased pressures of the times, amidst the calamities, the crises, and the tragedies that befall us. We seek to be part of communities of wholeness, reconciliation, caring, and justice.

We seek to discover new meanings so we can live lives of value, purpose, significance, and understanding in the light of the gospel. The old meanings have passed away. New meanings are important for now and the time to come. We build on what has been, and we cannot live in what has been. We can live in what is and what will be.

We are intentional, not passive. This is not a time for being inert and inactive, allowing events to toss and turn us, now one way, now another. This is not a time for passiveness, whether it be in raising our children, helping our families, sharing in our vocation, advancing our community, or strengthening our world. We are not simply passive toward the tragic, sad events that come to us. We have a sense for where we are headed and that we can head toward the future. We live proactively and intentionally. We serve the community and the world proactively and intentionally. We advance and improve, grow and develop the way we lead in our lives.

A Sense of Balance

A sense of balance contributes to our sense of leadership over our lives.

Balance breeds balance. In productive, constructive situations, most of us share a sense of balance. We lead with balance. We provide insight and experience, wisdom and common sense. We share positively, personally, relationally. We help the group get along well, have good fun and good times together. We live our lives and share our sense of leadership with steadiness, stability, and balance.

Excess breeds excess. What gets most of us in trouble in times of anxiety is that we respond in excess. It is not usually a weakness that causes us the difficulty. What gets us into difficulty is that some strength shows up in excess. Our sense of leadership, shared with balance, is productive and helpful. When we respond in excess, our response becomes unproductive and destructive.

To be sure, in anxiety-producing situations, it is more difficult to share a sense of balance.

"Dad, can I borrow the keys to the car tonight?" It was the first time I heard those words as a parent. It was a Friday. Our older son had just achieved his driver's license. With considerable enthusiasm, he asked for the keys to the car. My anxiety level soared.

Mostly, our anxiety level rolls along like the gentle, moving waves of an ocean current. There is some rise and fall, but overall we are fairly steady and mostly calm. When some new idea comes along, our anxiety level soars. We often reject a new idea not because we disagree with it—the idea is likely worthwhile. But the new idea has stirred our anxiety level. We reject it to get our anxiety level back down to normal.

My words just came out: "No, your mother and I plan to use the car tonight." The words just came out. The words were there even before I could think about the question. I'm not sure we really had planned to use the car. It was just the first thing that came to mind. Then I thought to myself, "What am I doing here? I taught him to drive. He passed the test with a grade of 100." So I said, "Well, you can have the keys to the car. You can't have the car, but you can have the keys." You could tell by the look on his face that it was not a helpful response.

I thought to myself, "He is a responsible person. He has demonstrated his ability to drive." I began to think of a variety of rules and regulations, conditions and stipulations, like "You can only drive within ten blocks of the house"; "You cannot drive over thirty miles a hour"; "You must be in by seven thirty."

I was still trying to deal with my high anxiety level. The rules and regulations were really my way of trying to assure myself all would be well.

Happily, I kept all those rules to myself. Finally, I amended what I'd said: "Here are the keys to the car. You can use the car. Have fun. Have a good time." I confess that as I watched him drive away in our car my anxiety level soared again. Julie reassured me all would be well. It was.

In anxiety-producing situations, when our anxiety level soars, we sometimes head to immediate rejection. In excess, we say no too quickly. This frequently breeds excessive resistance on the part of the other person. Our excessive behavior creates in the other person an excessive reaction. When one person in a group heads to any excess, it tends to create excessive responses in other persons in the group.

Johnny, a remarkable six-year-old boy, active and energetic, wanted to go outside. It was raining just a little, hardly a sprinkle. The babysitter who was staying with him that Thursday quickly said, "No, it's raining out." His voice slightly louder and more insistent, Johnny responded, "It's not raining that hard. I'm going out anyway." The babysitter matched the rising loudness of Johnny's voice, plus just a little louder: "Oh, no you are not, young man. You are going to stay right here."

Louder still, Johnny responded, "You can't make me stay inside. I'm going out right now." He started toward the door. The babysitter's voice was now louder and more strident still: "You'd better watch out. I'll make you go to timeout. You won't get any dessert for supper. You'll have to go to bed early." Johnny was now screaming at the top of his lungs: "I don't care. I'm going outside. You can't stop me." The babysitter, with stronger lungs and determination, shouted even louder: "All right, young man, march right up to your room. You are in timeout. There is no dessert for you tonight."

Excess breeds excess. One person heads to the excess of quick rejection and refusal. The move to excess in one person creates a move to excess in the other person. One excess feeds on another excess. Before long, the matter gets quickly out of hand.

Two days later, Johnny's grandmother found herself in the same predicament. Johnny, with amazing energy and liveliness, declared he wanted to go outside. It was raining just a little, hardly a sprinkle. Having heard of the sequence that had transpired two days earlier from both Johnny's mother and Johnny, his grandmother whispered, "You can go out later. It's raining outside now." His voice slightly lower, Johnny whispered, "It's not raining that hard. I want to go out anyway." Lowering her voice to the quietest of whispers, Johnny's grandmother said, "Let's play this game now and we'll go out later." In an even quieter whisper, Johnny said, "All right, Grandmother."

What we learn is this: when we want other persons to behave with balance, not excess, we need to behave with balance, and those around us are sure to frequently find their way to some form of balance as well.

We are not locked into a pattern of excess. It may be true that, for the present moment, excess is a frequent way you respond in times of anxiety. You can unlearn that pattern of excess. If you can learn an unhelpful, unproductive pattern of excess—which in fact requires considerable emotional energy both to learn and to maintain—you can learn to replace it with a helpful, constructive pattern of balance.

Balance breeds balance. When one person in a group heads to balance, shares a sense of steadiness and stability, that creates in others people who are steady and stable. Balance is contagious. Others begin to share their insight and experience, wisdom and common sense. A good-natured, harmonious spirit pervades the group. The move to balance in one person creates a move to balance in others. The art, in times of anxiety, is to share your leadership with balance, not excess. The stronger the balance, the better you lead your life.

Rediscovering Power

A sense of power contributes to our sense of leadership over our lives.

We lead whole, healthy lives as we have some sense of power in relation to our own life and destiny. Regrettably, many people increasingly sense that the decisions that affect their lives and shape their destinies are made somewhere else by someone else, and they can't quite figure out who, why, when, where. They develop a pervasive sense of powerlessness. God invites us to rediscover power in our own lives.

There is a trend toward dislocation of power. Over the past many years, power shifted from local to regional, and from regional to national locations. It was hard to find where the decisions were actually being made. Even today, when you go down to the courthouse to transact a simple bit of business, you are told to go to the new courthouse annex. There, you are directed up to the second floor, third door on the right, where you visit with a pleasant, gray-haired lady. She tells you that this business used to be done there, but it is now done in the state capitol.

You write the state capitol. You get a letter back saying it used to be done there, but that it is now done in a regional office. You write the regional office, and you get a letter back that says it is now done in Washington, D.C. You write them. You get a letter back that suggests you go down to the new courthouse annex, second floor, third door on the right.

You are told a pleasant, gray-haired lady will help you. Lots of people in our time experience a profound sense of this dislocation of power as it relates to their lives and destinies.

The sense of powerlessness is pervasive, troubling, and destructive. The symptoms are apathy and anger. I am frequently invited to help groups think through the apathy of their members. It is not as simple as member apathy toward the group. When one looks closely, one discovers that in all spheres and sectors of their lives—in the religious, social, civic, communal, vocational, educational, economic, recreational, family, and political arenas—there is a sense of apathy.

Powerlessness yields apathy. Power produces action. When people have more power, they express more action and less apathy. It is not as simple as saying, "If people only had more commitment, they wouldn't be apathetic." If people sense they have power over their own lives and destinies, then, to be sure, they exercise ownership and action.

Another symptom of powerlessness is anger. It is not accidental that many people in our time are angry. The more powerless people feel, the angrier they become. The more power people sense they have over their own lives, the less angry they are.

People bring their anger to their family. Many times the anger comes from somewhere else in their lives. They displace their anger in their family. Where else can they share their anger? Indeed, they hope surely that their family understands the roots of their anger, and loves and cares for them, even as they express their displaced anger.

Sometimes, around a dinner table, people vent anger over the most trivial thing. Others in the family do not always understand what is happening. Frequently, people are displacing anger from some other sector of their lives. They are doing so in the one place they hope people understand and accept them, namely, their family. It is, for that moment in time, safer to shout one's anger over family finances at home than it is to shout one's anger to one's boss at work over the tenuousness of the job, the long hours, and the unfairness of the salary. Displaced anger is an important clue to the pervasive sense of powerlessness that many people feel in our culture.

Sometimes, people are rightfully angry in their family, when their family has lost its sense of wholeness and health, compassion and hope, when it has become involved in destructive patterns of behavior. At the same time, it is important to understand that anger is a symptom of the sense of powerlessness people feel in their lives.

In our time, the drive toward local sources of power is best understood as people's effort to recover some sense of power over their own life and destiny. The demand for power is strong, and growing stronger. People want some sense of power over their own lives and destinies. The art is to discover constructive, creative ways to recover power to shape one's own life and destiny. There is promise in our time. Today, people are discovering constructive groups that help them claim a fuller sense of power as they move forward to lead a whole, healthy future.

In every local community, there are constructive groups that are helping persons claim a fuller sense of power as they move forward to lead a whole, healthy future. You benefit in your own life as you participate in one or more of these constructive groups. John participates in Alcoholics Anonymous. Mary participates in Al-Anon. Sally has found a professional women's group. Bill has found an active business group. Beverly has discovered resources in her support group. Tony has found help in an informal men's group in his congregation. All of them have a fuller sense of power in their own lives.

The Capacity to Deal with Conflict

The capacity to deal with conflict contributes to our sense of leadership over our lives. As we move through this life, we experience conflicts. We begin to develop our capacity to deal with conflict when we come to understand that some conflict is simply part of life. Conflict is present in the best of families. It may be as mundane as two people arguing over squeezing the toothpaste tube from the end or in the middle, or it may be as major as two people disagreeing over what part of the country to live in or what vocation to pursue.

In the best of families, we have our fair share of conflict. Even with people who deeply love one another and have lived together as husband and wife for many years, there is occasionally a conflict. Sometimes, one brother has a tendency to beat up another brother. Two sisters don't speak to one another for a period of years. At the family reunions, they are careful to avoid one another. They make it a point to get to the table, at different times, where the food is spread out, for fear they might have to exchange even a simple hello.

Sometimes, two friends who love one another shout at each other, or shout and then sulk. Sometimes, one brother is at his father's house, taking those mementos that he just knows his father would want him to have, even as the other brother is at the funeral home making the arrangements for their father's funeral. Conflict is part of life.

When we have not learned some capacity to deal with conflict, we feel a sense of being battered to and fro, hither and yon. Conflict does not need to control us. We do not need to become victims of the conflicts that come. We lead our lives in whole, healthy ways, as we develop our capacity to deal with conflict.

What distinguishes the best of families is not the absence of conflict but their capacity to deal with conflict. The only people I know who don't have conflict are the people buried in the nearest cemetery, and sometimes I'm not so sure about them. When I walk by late at night, I hear the mutterings and the murmurings. Conflict is present in the best of families.

Some people try to deny conflict, and their very denial makes it more difficult for them to develop any capacity to deal with it. Some people acknowledge conflict exists but seek to repress it. Some people—fortunately not many—seem to thrive on conflict. If one is not brewing, they figure out how to start one. They have, for whatever reasons, learned a pattern of behavior in which they seem almost to go out of their way to create conflict around them. Neither denying nor repressing nor stirring conflict is helpful.

What helps is to accept, with some degree of calmness and serenity, that conflict will come. This quiet acceptance helps us not be alarmed, apprehensive, or frightened when conflict does arise. As a consequence, we are able to deal with the conflict more constructively and creatively.

We develop our capacity to deal with conflict as we to come to understand that differences of priorities can engender conflict. Mostly, people do get along pretty well with one another. At the same time, there are sometimes disagreements over the primary priorities for the present and the future. Two partners in business have different priorities. One wants the business to succeed as a small, strong business, free of debt. The other partner wants the business to expand into a large national organization, even as that means acquiring considerable debt to finance the expansion. They have been friends since grade school. They started the business with much optimism and goodwill. They were moderately successful. Their emerging difference of priorities almost cost them their lifelong friendship.

A father wanted his son to go to college. He insisted his son go. He never had the chance to go himself, so his son must go to college. The son hoped to be an auto mechanic. Countless arguments and conflicts ensued. The arguments lasted late into the night. Years passed. The son found his way to being one of the best auto mechanics in the area. Finally, the father and son came to peace with one another. The son knew his strengths best.

We learn to deal with conflict as we to come to discern that differences of process can engender conflict. Some people do not understand this. They mostly insist on things being done their way. The consequence is that they are frequently involved in a conflict of process. We discover ways forward as we honor our distinctive, differing ways of doing things. Sometimes, people agree on the priorities but differ on the process with which to achieve the priorities. They go about doing things differently. They concur on the end but have differing means for achieving the end.

Parents and youths frequently agree that to achieve reasonably good grades is a helpful priority. But they also frequently disagree on the process for achieving those grades. The parents, who do things steadily, routinely, regularly, day by day, insist that their son or daughter study two hours each night. The son or daughter studies best in short, intensive bursts near the time at hand. There are countless arguments over study hours, to the extent that the real priority is almost lost in the conflict over process. Once they mutually discover that they have distinctive ways of going about the same priority, they come to a sense of peace about the way forward.

We advance our ability to deal with conflict as we to come to understand that the gospel can occasion conflict. Sometimes, as the grace and compassion central to the gospel are shared, conflict does ensue. This conflict may occur within the individual or between two or more people. Now, it is not true that when there is conflict one can automatically assume that the gospel is being shared. Some make the mistake of assuming that simply because they are involved in conflict they are, therefore, sharing the gospel. Just because there is conflict does not mean the gospel is being shared.

But sometimes the gospel itself engenders conflict. That certainly is part of the biblical message. We are invited to leave off old ways and come to new ways. We experience tension and conflict as we sort through which values are the values we want to live through in this life's pilgrimage. We may find ourselves in conflict with people who have adopted values different from the ones we are pursuing.

Wherever the gospel is richly and fully shared, people struggle to choose the direction for their life and destiny. That tension, that conflict, that decisive invitation to a new way is important. It is vital that this spirit of conflict be amply and fully present in our lives, so we can develop into whole, healthy persons.

Consider the conflicts present in your life, particularly those that are decisive for you. Some may be a best-of-families conflicts. Some may be conflicts of priorities or of process. Some conflicts may, appropriately and importantly, be expressions of the gospel's inviting you to new life. Be open to the ways in which the dynamic of conflict affects your present life and your future.

Several suggestions help. First, if you find yourself involved in some conflict, ask yourself the question, "Is this conflict important?" This question saves you much time, energy, and emotion. Many times the answer is, "No, this is not important." Move on. Do not allow yourself to get sucked into a conflict that is not important. Some conflicts are not worth the time, trouble, or energy. They are incidental to living a whole, healthy life.

Second, when you decide a conflict is in fact important, then be sure you are taking care of the things you need to be doing. Keep your own life in order. Say to yourself, "My side of the street is clean." Regardless of what other people are doing in the midst of the conflict, you are acting thoughtfully and responsibly.

Third, try neither to give nor receive offense. As best you can, behave in such a way that you are not offending people around you. This does not mean that you become placating. It does mean that you behave thoughtfully. Do not intentionally offend or cause harm to someone else. Likewise, do not take personal offense from someone else's action or remark. In some instances, you might consider the source and let the remark go. If we allow ourselves to be offended by someone, we get off track and deal poorly with the conflict at hand.

Fourth, when you are moving in a healthy direction, hold to your course. If someone tries to intervene in an unhealthy way, do not get distraught. In sailboat racing, there is considerable competition and conflict. Sometimes, when rounding a buoy, the skipper of the blue sailboat tries to force the green sailboat off course. The blue skipper who is forcing the issue is doing so in violation of the rules of right-of-way in sailing. The green skipper who is being forced is encouraged to follow the rules of the road, to maintain the heading on which he is sailing.

When some conflict is forcing you to head in an unhealthy direction, do not get distracted by the conflict. The helpful thing you can do is to hold to the healthy direction in which you are headed. In time of conflict, maintain a constructive way forward. John Ruskin once wrote, "The highest reward for a person's toil is not what they get for it, but what they become by it." Some wise unknown person once said, "Success is more attitude than aptitude." To paraphrase Romans 12:18, "If possible, so far as it depends on you, be at peace with all persons."

We *lead* our lives in whole, healthy ways as we are proactive and intentional, share a sense of balance, rediscover power, and have the capacity to deal with conflict.

○

Hope is stronger than memory.
  We are the people of hope.
The cradle of Bethlehem is stronger than the thrones of kings.
  We are the people of Bethlehem.
The newborn Savior is stronger than the armies of the world.
  We are the people of new life.
God leads us in new paths of leadership and mission.
  We are leaders in God's mission.
Light is stronger than darkness.
  We are the people of light.
    We are the Christmas people.
      We are the people of wonder and joy.
      Amen.

8

SIMPLICITY

MARION WAS A GOOD MOTHER. She had just given birth to a beautiful baby. Healthy and happy. The birth had gone well. Marion's third daughter. The doctor (among the best in the country) was pleased. The hospital staff (with the finest facilities and equipment) were pleased. The day for going home had come.

The war was on. Marion's husband, Joe, was in Philadelphia. He was ready to be shipped overseas, to the war in Europe. Everyone was doing his or her part to win the war. Uncle Welcome and Aunt Teat had gone to the hospital to bring Marion and the new baby home.

Marion was getting in the car, which was pulled close to the hospital door so she would not have to walk so far. It was a happy time. Her favorite nurse was wishing her well, holding the door for her, helping her into the car. Marion asked Aunt Teat to take the baby. She settled into her seat, sighed, and died.

The doctor said it was a blood clot. No warning. They took Marion back up. Quickly. Nothing could be done. It happened so fast. The baby went home. Marion stayed at the hospital—her body did. Later, people remembered Marion had felt faint going down to the car. In the excitement of the new baby and of going home, the feeling had passed, for a moment.

Joe was overdue in Europe, but he rushed home from the staging area in Philadelphia on the death of his wife. There was much to attend to, arrangements to be made, the funeral service to be worked out, grieving and mourning to be shared. He was shipping out in a few days. He had to get back. Joe had a new baby and two older daughters, two and four in age. What to do?

Eileen, Marion's sister, had two sons, ages three and five. Her husband was headed to the Pacific to fight the war in that theater. Arta was forty-eight years of age at the time. She was Eileen and Marion's mother. Eileen and Arta took hold and raised the three girls and two boys during the war. Their gift of love was remarkable.

Life is complex. Wonderful events happen: there is the birth of a new baby. Tragic events happen: there is the death of the mother. Amidst the complexities of life, we do well when, as best we can, we focus on the simple basics. This is not easy to do. The pace of life, the rush of events is rapid and complicated. Good surprises, convolutions, tragedies abound. As our good friend Sarah has wisely observed, "It's just when complexity really gets out of hand that one has an excellent opportunity to see the simplicity at its heart: for example, feed the baby, everything else can wait." Keep life simple. Live one day at a time—one hour at a time.

Making Decisions

One key, one possibility, for a whole, healthy life is a life of simplicity. We live constructive lives when, amidst the complications, changes, confusions, and difficulties that abound, we develop the resources for a simple life:

- A healthy approach in making decisions
- The ability to deal with change
- A balanced capacity in gathering things
- Working well with others

With these components present in our lives, we are able to enjoy a single-minded life of simple comforts and moderation. Life is less ostentatious. We are not drawn to extravagance and pretentiousness. The vanities and affectations around us do not tempt us. Our lives have an informality and naturalness that fit with who we are.

One resource for developing a life of simplicity is a healthy approach in making decisions. Decision making, when we do it reasonably well, focuses on what is important. The more complex life is, the more crucial it is that we develop our capacity to focus on what is important. Perhaps you are aware of this helpful principle:

> Twenty percent of the things we do yield 80 percent of the results we achieve.

One way to understand the principle is this: two out of ten things we do yield 80 percent of our results, accomplishments, and achievements. The art of a life of simplicity is deciding which are the 20 percenters.

The twelve keys for a whole, healthy life are 20 percenters. Among the twelve, the ones you expand as current strengths and add as new strengths are 20 percenters for you. Focus on these. They are decisive in developing a whole, healthy life. They are central to your future.

Conversely, 80 percent of the things we do yield 20 percent of the results we achieve. Many decisions in life are 80 percenters. We need to make them, and move on. We do them with dignity and decorum, and they achieve 20 percent of our results, accomplishments, and achievements.

Life gets complex, instead of simple, if two things happen. First, we do not know which of the twelve keys are the 20 percenters, which are genuinely important for us. When that occurs, our tendency is to turn everything we do into a 20 percenter. Now, life is really complex.

Second, we spend too much time, energy, and effort on the 80 percenters. We may have discerned which, for us, are the 20 percenters and which are the 80 percenters, but we make the mistake of investing too much time in the 80 percenters. In a life of simplicity, we focus on those few among the twelve keys important for our own growth and development. We let less important matters resolve themselves, or we spend a modest amount of time on them. Ralph Waldo Emerson said, "Common sense is genius dressed in its working clothes." We use our common sense.

Healthy decisions are made with a spirit of grace and peace, not anxiety and fear. God invites us to live a simple life, not a fearful life. Jesus said, ". . . fear not . . ." (Luke 12:7). Sometimes, we become anxious and afraid. Anxiety is the ancestor of fear. Anxiety turns into fear. Fear is the ancestor of anger. When we have fear, we become angry. The deeper our anxiety and fear, the louder our anger, the stronger our rage.

Decisions made in anxiety, fear, anger, and rage are less than constructive. They are the decisions for which we get to apologize later. Healthy decision making is not anxious and angry, filled with fear and panic. A healthy approach to decision making is constructive and forward moving, not convoluted and tangled, not drawn out more than needed. Decisions made with a sense of grace and peace, calm and confidence tend to be constructive decisions.

Sometimes, we make decisions quickly. Now. It is done. Other times, we make decisions in a protracted, taking-our-time, we-will-know-when-it-is-the-right-time approach to deciding. Some decisions do take time. It is not the length of time, short or long, that is central. Nor is it the specific number of steps in one's thought process. We sometimes get lost in the maze of our own thinking, almost forgetting what it was we were trying to decide.

We occasionally postpone, putting off—then putting off again—the moment of deciding. On other occasions we approach a decision indirectly; we come around behind, then move up on the decision. We look back and wonder, "Now, when and how did I make that decision?" We sort of make the decision hardly realizing we were doing so. It doesn't matter how we make the decision. It matters *which* decisions. Healthy decisions focus on the 20 percenters. We make them with grace and peace. We invest an appropriate amount of time in making them.

Dealing with Change

We lead simpler lives as we develop the capacity to deal with change. If we do not deal well with change, then life becomes hectic and confusing, complicated and tangled. The more changes in our lives, the more important it is that we develop our capacity to deal with change.

Consider all of the changes with which we deal. The rise or fall of the economy, major cultural developments, issues of war and peace across the planet, the building of new homes in our area, a six-lane highway that has shaped in new ways the traffic patterns of a community, the opening of a factory or the closing of one. Economic, social, political, vocational, recreational, religious, demographic, and geographic changes all have a strong impact on all of us.

Importantly, the changes happening in your own family and informal groupings contribute much to the dynamics of your life. Marion died in childbirth. A new baby was born. Eileen and Arta raised the five children during the war. One kind of change is that some persons are born and some persons die in our family.

A second kind of change is the coming and leaving of people. I remember the Sunday when Bill first came to church. He was chief of the volunteer fire department in the community. He was a generous person. He was also known to have problems with drinking. He was the best leader when there was a fire, but for some people he was unacceptable the rest of the time because of his drinking.

That Sunday as he walked in we were sitting down from singing the first hymn. There was a hush. No one seemed quite sure what to do. No one was quite sure he belonged there. Then big, gentle Orville, leader in the community, principal of the school, mentor to many, got up out of his pew, went back down the aisle, and put his arms around Bill. Bill was home. The congregation accepted Bill, and the congregation was never quite the same from that day forward because of the arrival of that one person.

I was helping a church in the mountains of north Georgia. In the choir that Sunday was a sixteen-year-old girl, clearly very pregnant under her choir robe. She had become pregnant, unmarried. In that part of the planet, the stigma is strong. Her family had turned her out. She lived now here, now there, in the early months of her pregnancy. One Sunday morning, halfway through her pregnancy, desperate, she came to church. Amazingly, the congregation took her in.

Look at the change the congregation went through as they took her in. They overcame, in themselves, all sorts of conventional injunctions and legalisms about never being pregnant outside of wedlock, let alone at sixteen, let alone without the support of one's family. With the arrival of that new person, the congregation became richly and fully a changed, new congregation.

A third kind of change happens as people grow and develop. As they grow in their own life's pilgrimage, their contributions to their own family and friends develop as well. Gene was an excellent carpenter. He liked to do things with his hands; he was good with tools. Gene was also an ardent student of the Gospel. It expanded profoundly his understanding of the meaning and purpose of life.

The parables of God as loving father instilled in him a vision of how he could become a more loving husband and father. As he began to manifest these changes, Gene found himself led to be of greater service in his community. His quiet, steady growth and development became a strong encouragement to many.

Through Gene, many people began to discover new ways in which their lives could have value and significance, meaning and purpose.

As you grow in your own life, you will be, even more fully than you are now, a source of growth for the people around you. As you develop in this life's pilgrimage, your contributions affect, in healthy ways, those around you. As you advance your capacity to deal with change—as you learn to deal with the changes brought on by birth and death, the coming and leaving of people, the growing and developing of the persons in your life—you lead a life of simplicity.

Gathering Things

One resource for developing a life of simplicity is a balanced capacity in gathering things. The more things we acquire from the plethora of mail-order catalogues that find their way into our lives, the more problems we now have acquired:

○ How and where to store it

○ How to protect it

○ Whether to insure it and for how much

○ How to organize it

○ How to maintain it

Once these dilemmas have been worked out, then we can also figure out how to use and enjoy it. It is not accidental that the two happiest times in a boat owner's life are buying the boat and selling the boat. In between, it is said, he pours money into a hole in the water.

Acquisition of things contributes to our enjoyment of life. Much of our gathering of things is through impulse buying. Impulse acquisition is a short-term, quick-closure, immediate-satisfaction activity that helps us feel we have accomplished something. We have. Someone once said a house is a roof under which we store our junk and try to keep it dry.

We know impulse buying well. We go to the store, with our shopping list made out. We know the few things we need to purchase. Time passes. We have fun in the store. We get to the checkout line and we discover our shopping cart is filled with items that were not on our list. Sometimes we wonder how they got there.

We gather things, on impulse and fancy, and we have fun doing so. With some of things we collect, we cannot even remember what they are for. A good friend of mine, Merrill Douglas, has a saying: "Clutter expands to fill the space available." Another friend of mine had a work-bench stacked high with piles and piles of this and that. He thought, "If I get another workbench, my workshop will be better organized." Now he has two workbenches stacked high with piles and piles of this and that. Sometimes when we look closely around our house, we wonder where all the stuff came from.

Life is more than acquiring things, however notable, useful, attractive, pleasurable, and comforting they may be. As we share in the richness of God's grace and discover the fullness of God's hope, the *things* we need take on a lesser value. Our belongings do not give us a sense of belonging. Life is not about possessions, however reassuring—albeit fleetingly—they may be. Life is about the qualities of whole, healthy living.

We gather things because it is part of the fun of living. We know what we gather has its relative, rightful place in the larger picture. Our sense of value and worth as persons is in who we are and whose we are, not in what we have accumulated. We know the center of our being is more than the collection of things we have acquired. Knowing this, we can simplify our life.

Working Together

One resource for developing a life of simplicity is a capacity to work together. The more complex life is, the more important it is that we learn how to work with one another. When we try to do everything by ourselves, then life becomes complex. We lose the strengths and competencies, the wisdom and common sense, the energy and support of those around us. We become weary and tired from trying to go it alone. Working together, with trust and cooperation, we have the ability to move forward.

Life is simpler when we trust those with whom we live and work. Trust breeds trust. As we share our trust with people around us, we become more fully trusted by them. Trust is mutual. We *share* trust: we both give and receive trust. Our capacity to work together grows.

Mistrust breeds mistrust. As we mistrust persons, they began to mistrust us. If we mistrust even those we love, then life becomes complex. To be sure, some persons behave in ways that they do not easily engender our trust. Indeed, their behavior suggests caution rather than trust. I do think we are wise about the persons we trust. At the same time, a climate of mistrust diminishes our capacity to share and work together.

If we trust people, two things usually happen. First, they trust us. Second, they act in trustworthy ways with us and with one another. If we mistrust persons, two things frequently happen. First, they mistrust us. Second, they act in untrustworthy ways with us and with one another. It is true that sometimes, when we trust a person, the individual betrays our trust. We have a choice. We can trust people and sometimes be disappointed. We can mistrust them and hardly ever be disappointed. People tend to live either forward or downward to the trust we place in them.

When we trust ourselves, we are in a healthier position to trust others. Sometimes, when we do not trust others, it is because we do not trust ourselves. Trust starts with our trusting ourselves to live constructive lives. If we trust ourselves, we are more easily able to trust those around us, and we work well together.

Life is simpler when we cooperate with one another. If we try to go it alone, rigid and unbending, then life becomes complex. Trust and cooperation go together. The more trust we share, the more cooperative we can be with one another. Likewise, the more cooperative we are, the more easily we can trust.

Cooperation breeds cooperation. Our spirit of cooperation encourages others to discover their spirit of cooperation. We both share and receive cooperation. We develop a healthy working relationship with people.

In our time, we are more likely to live a simpler life as we work together. To be sure, there are some things each of us can successfully do alone. Not everything needs to be done together with someone. At the same time, given the complexities of this time, in working together we are more likely to move forward in ways that contribute to our living a simple life.

We can work together as a team. Each person brings distinctive gifts and competencies, but there are no higher or lower gifts. In this time, people are not drawn to groups preoccupied with keeping some persons on pedestals. We are—together—God's people. We share and work together in the spirit of a team.

We may have a team leader, but no autocratic, dictatorial boss. There is no chasm between the team leader and the team. When we work constructively together, it is frequently hard to discern who the team leader is. Given the particular situation, the sense of who the team leader is varies from one person to another on the team. As we work together, we have just enough structure that we can have fun sharing and working together. What structure we have is relative, dynamic, and flexible. It is not absolute, static, or rigid. It is grassroots.

Working together as a team looks like a M*A*S*H team at the front lines. We pitch in and help where we can and in ways we can. We trust one another and cooperate as we work together. Only the character of Frank in "M*A*S*H" wanted to function in a rigid, static, top-down, organizational way. A team has more the structure of an excellent fast break on the basketball court than a neat, tidy, carefully constructed game plan. The structure is creative and improvisational, not routine and rigid.

We are drawn to a team, not a rigid structure. We know a team trusts us helpfully and encouragingly. We know a rigid structure does not trust us. Rather, it seeks to keep us in our place. We give our lives, deeply and compassionately, to teams. We share trust and cooperation. We discover how we can work together. We help one another.

We live rich, full lives as we develop a healthy approach in making decisions, advance our ability to deal with change, have a balanced capacity in gathering things, and work together. Life is more simply lived.

○

Go and share.
   Go with God's encouragement.
      Go with God's reassurance.
         Go and live a life of simplicity.
The great banquet of God's grace has begun.
   The wedding feast of God's hope has come.
Go with laughing wonder.
   Go with tears of joy,
      with the drenching rains of grace,
         with the tumbling waters of good news.
Go and share the resurrection of compassion and hope.
   Live well. Live simply.
      God is with you. Amen.

9

JOY

I AM SURE heaven is more fun because Mimi is there. She lived to be nearly ninety-seven years of age. Across my years of knowing her, nearly half a century, what I remember most are her smile, her laughter, her gay, free spirit. She knew how to have fun.

Not all of us have learned the art of having fun. We are sometimes too serious, too task-oriented, too much involved in this achievement or that accomplishment, too much in a hurry to succeed at this or that.

Mimi raised two girls, mostly by herself, during the darkest part of the Depression. Then, after she had lived nearly half a century, she pitched in to help raise her five grandchildren.

She loved to play the piano, to sing, to share games, to have fun. Even when bits of newspaper had to be used to fill the holes in the bottom of her shoes, even when there was only one outfit in the house for each person to wear, even when the food on the table was scarce, she could have fun.

My dad has fun. He is known for his honesty and integrity, his wisdom and hard work. He is respected for all he has accomplished in his life. People write him often in appreciation for some act of kindness and thoughtfulness he did for them, whether years ago or in recent times. In his growing-up years, Dad earned, for his tousled, red hair, the nickname Red. With affection, his earliest friends called him Red.

Dad and Mom moved from our old hometown long ago. Some thirty years after they moved away, they went back for a reunion. While at the reunion, they made their way to their favorite restaurant. It was known for its wonderful food and as a gathering place for the whole community. As they walked in—thirty years had come and gone since they had moved away—one person raised his voice above the pleasant, busy conversations going on at the tables and said, "Hey, there's Red! He's the most honest man I know."

There followed rushed, warm greetings, hugs and kisses, welcoming words and embraces. There were stories upon stories. People said later they hadn't laughed so much in a long time. It was one of those evenings of joy and good fun people remember for years.

Dad is known for his ability to have fun. His laughter, his kidding, his way of seeing a good joke, even in the midst of tragic events cause him to be loved and appreciated. His good humor has seen him, and many of his family and friends, through some otherwise very dark times.

There is a gentle spirit to my mother's way of doing things. There is a kindness and thoughtfulness in her life that is rarer than gold or precious gems. She shares her compassion quietly and steadily, ever mindful of the needs of those about her.

Growing up, she never had much. Indeed, as I have listened more closely in recent years, I know now it is fairer to say that she had next to nothing in her growing up years. Her father died suddenly while she was very young. I never knew my grandfather on my mother's side. She and her sister were devoted to one another. With their mother, Mimi, they were all each other had. The early years of Mom's life were scarcer than scarce. Yet they knew how to have fun together.

I remember my grandmother on my father's side. Her warm, wonderful oatmeal cookies were the best ever. Many in the family have tried to duplicate them, using the recipe she so readily shared, to no avail. Her quiet manner, gentle ways, well-kept home, Sunday meals around the table of food she lovingly prepared, all of these are fond memories. Mostly, I remember her shy smile, light laughter, and joyous spirit.

My grandfather. There was always a twinkle in his eye. He knew how to have fun. We would be sitting on their enclosed front porch, my grandfather, my grandmother, and I. Frequently I would visit them on my own. It was a good walk from our home to theirs. We would be talking about something. A slow smile would spread across his face, his eyes would light up, the twinkle in his eye would become a beam of fun, joy, laughter. He would share some wonderful story, mostly now dim in my memory. What I do remember is that the story would express the joy of living, of family, of being together.

God surrounds us with people who know how to have fun, who, even amidst the dark depressions, sad events of life, deep tragedies that befall them, know the joy of life, have a capacity for fun, to laugh and carry on, to have a good time. It is an art worth our learning.

God wants us to know the joy of life, to share in the laughter of good fun and good times. God gives us people who have discovered how to share joy and laughter so that we might discover this precious gift, that our lives might be whole and healthy.

A Sense of Wonder About Life

One key, one possibility, for a whole, healthy life is joy. God invites us to a life of joy, not sorrow. We are at our best when, amidst the sadness, tenseness, distrust, and disappointments that abound, we discover the sources for a life of joy:

- o A sense of wonder
- o Learning to relax and have fun
- o The ability to express our feelings
- o Living in and trusting God

One source of joy is a sense of wonder. We have a sense of wonder that we are alive, that we live and breathe, move and love. There is extraordinary wonder in simply knowing that we live. Further, we live in awe of the grace of God in our lives. Not only are we alive but we are loved by God extraordinarily, far beyond anything we might anticipate or expect. Sometimes, we do not love ourselves. We look down on ourselves, think more poorly of ourselves than we have a right to, suffer from low self-esteem. Even then, God loves us. This is an amazing wonder.

In recent years, really in the last twenty-five years, we have been discovering the immensity of the universe. We stand in awe of all creation. Psalm 19:1 (NASB) expresses the spirit of wonder: "The heavens are telling of the glory of God; and their expanse [their immensity] is declaring the work of His hands." We develop a sense of amazement and reverence for life—and all creation—for its immensity and variety.

We live in a universe that stretches our comprehension. Its immensity of light years, millions upon millions of galaxies, stars and solar systems beyond number, more than the sands of all the oceans and shores, testify to the joy and wonder of God. The universe sings praises to its creator, God. We stand in awe and wonder.

Relaxing and Having Fun

There is an ancient saying: "Live well. Laugh often. Love much." The second part of the saying suggests that we understand laughter and having fun deeply and profoundly. To be sure, we have times of fun that are lighthearted and almost frivolous. Life is sufficiently precious that we should cherish even more these light moments. There are also occasions when we relax and have fun deeply and profoundly.

The capacity to learn how to relax and have fun is an extraordinary gift you can give to yourself. Indeed, as we relax and have fun, we give this gift to all of those around us. Laughter is contagious. Relaxing relaxes those around us. When we have fun, those around us have fun.

We are too often tense and tight, nervous and anxious, mostly over things that, in the long haul of life, amount to very little. We allow ourselves to be distracted by petty matters that are of minor consequence. We become preoccupied with these small difficulties, and in the process we become tense and tight, unable to relax.

We help ourselves relax when we have a few objectives that are specific and concrete, realistic and achievable, with solid time horizons. If we create too many goals, set them too high, expect them to be accomplished too soon, then we become overwhelmed, unable to relax and have fun. As we keep our eye on a few objectives, looking to God, we can more easily relax.

If we do not know the few goals that count, then everything becomes an important and urgent goal, to be accomplished now. We end up with too many goals, with too little time, and we take our eyes off the few objectives that in fact count. We become distracted, busily seeking to do too much too soon, and we are tense and tight.

Mostly, we worry over matters that are minor and inconsequential. Or we worry about matters over which we have no control. When you worry, worry over a worry worth worrying about. Worry about something worthwhile. Worry over something you can do something about. Then, having worried in a worthwhile way, relax. When you go to bed at night, and cannot quite go to sleep for worrying over something, ask yourself: "Is this a worry worth worrying about?" Then ask yourself: "Is this a worry I can do something about?" Then, relax and go to sleep.

The worries that are worth worrying about and that you can do something about can be tackled when you are in the freshest, best position to do something about them: in the morning. The other, lesser worries, give over to God. God will worry about those for you. Let them go. Learn to whisper, "Oh, God . . ." and let it be a whispered prayer. When you feel you have more piled on you than you can do, you help yourself get it all into perspective by whispering, "Oh, God. . . ." Let God fill in the blank. This reminds you that you are not alone, and that you are never asked to do more than you and God together can handle. So call on your silent Partner—this God with the amazing sense of humor—to help you get beyond the current overwhelming situations so you can both enjoy the fun of it together.

Be at peace. Relax. Discover new ways you can have fun. For each worry worth really worrying about, that you can do something about, discover one new way you can have fun in this life. For each significant worry, find some significant way of having fun. Your life will have a sense of balance, health, and wholeness.

God laughs. The omnipotent, omniscient, all-powerful, all-knowing, saving Being-above-all-beings, the Holy, Lord God almighty, maker and ruler of all things laughs. Yes, God knows of our times of suffering. We have experienced times of suffering and pain, knowing that God is with us. We know also that God gives us new life. God's spirit is of joy and wonder. God is Christmas. God is Easter. God is Pentecost.

Jesus laughs. I have a copy of a picture of Jesus laughing. The laughter—you can see and feel it in the picture—is good-natured and gentle, understanding and joyful. Think of it. With all around him and all before him, Jesus laughs. He describes wedding feasts and great banquets. He shares wonder and joy, new life and hope.

A phrase came to me late one night, gently and invitingly, quietly and peacefully: "Relax, have fun, enjoy life, live in Christ." I have shared that phrase in seminars around the planet.

People share with me that they have put the phrase on their mirror, so they see it first thing in the morning. Pastors teach me that the phrase sits on their pulpit, and each Sunday, when they begin the service, they begin in this spirit. Countless persons share that this is their prayer as they go to bed at night. People describe how, in the midst of joyful events, the phrase comes to them. Many persons share how, in the midst of difficult times, these words see them through. As we learn how to relax and have fun, in the deepest sense possible, we are more able to live lives of joy, deeply and profoundly.

Expressing Feelings

A third source of joy is the ability to express our feelings. One of the helpful habits we can learn is the ability to give and receive feedback. This is a pattern of behavior that is helpful to us, to our loved ones, and to those around us.

It is interesting how life works.

The winds were becoming gusty. The waves had more of a chop. The thirty-six-foot sailboat we had rented for an afternoon's sail was due back at 5:00 P.M. The clouds in the southeast were becoming darker, more ominous. We had planned the afternoon as a relaxing, fun outing with our two young children, my mother, grandmother, and great aunt. But as we looked to the southeast, we could see a storm coming far off. Julie, who prefers fair-weather sailing, began to share her anxiety over the potentially threatening weather. We were sailing toward the southeast, directly toward the storm. She suggested that a change of course would put us in a better position to return to the harbor entrance when we wanted to go back. We would be closer to the harbor and could more easily reach our dock, particularly if the storm picked up speed in its approach.

By remarking about these weather signs in a conversational tone, she was able to communicate her rising concerns in a manner that gave alarm to neither the older women aboard nor the children. They continued to enjoy one another's company in the cabin below (they had volunteered to move below so as to not be in the way as we prepared to change course), totally oblivious to the problems we were encountering with the boat and the advancing weather.

Julie and I were able to stay calm, exchange our expressions of concern, and share mutual directions for trying to solve the obstacles we encountered as we tried to change course. We were able to do so without raising our voices or getting into anger, blame, or strife—to the extent that when we finally reached the dock, the children and the older women were unaware of the scope of the advancing endangerment we had all been in. Perhaps as remarkably, they were able to relax and have fun knowing that they were not in charge; they were along for the ride and didn't involve themselves in something they weren't responsible for, instead trusting the captains (us).

In a similar manner, we can learn to relax and have fun with our family and friends, knowing that we are not in charge of the big picture. In many respects, we are along for the ride, and we are in the care of a Captain Who is looking out for our well-being.

It is confusing. Sometimes, we are encouraged to share our feelings. Other times, we are encouraged to keep our feelings to ourselves. Then we are encouraged to share what is on our mind and in our heart, and later we are encouraged to keep our thoughts to ourselves. As a result, we may bottle our feelings up, keeping them to ourselves for days, even years, on end.

Then, in a rush of anger, an eruption of resentment, a surging of bitterness, they pour forth, like a dam breaking, the waters rushing to flood the town below. We share sharp words, hurtful words, bitter words. The words pour out in staccato fashion, abruptly, tumbling, not making sense, cascading forth from our mouths. The anger, the resentment, the bitterness, we wonder where all of this stuff has come from. We cannot seem to stop. Relentlessly, unceasingly, the words keep coming. In the midst of the torrent we know this rage of words is not an ability to give and receive feedback. We are out of control. We have lost it. We are at our worst.

One of the arts of living is to express our feelings constructively and helpfully, to share how we actually feel about something without, at the same time, doing so in a way that is harmful to those we love, without scolding and complaining, whining and lamenting. We allow our feelings to get the best of us. We go overboard. Sometimes, we keep our feelings inside. We bottle them up. We repress them. We clam up.

Then, some trigger event happens.

The pendulum swings wildly, rushingly to the other extreme. Before we know it, we are shouting, crying, intensely hissing, bitterly and hurtfully saying things that leap from our mouths; even as we try to trap the words before they escape, they rush forth, bringing even more words behind them.

There are too many words we wish had never escaped from our mouths. We are ashamed. There are too many deeds we wish we had never done. We are embarrassed. Then we have to figure out how to make amends, to apologize, to right the wrong that the words have caused, that *we* have caused.

We have learned a negative, hurtful way of sharing our feelings. There is nothing positive about that way. If we have figured out how to learn that way, then we can figure out a more helpful way. If we have learned a destructive habit, we can learn a constructive habit. With honor and integrity, we can share how we feel.

We can share constructive feelings of praise and thankfulness, appreciation and compassion: "Good job!" When we are anxious, we can share our anxiety without blaming those around us: "I'm concerned about the dark clouds ahead." When we are fearful, we can share our fears—without frightening those we love: "When I push the tiller. . . ." When we are angry, we can share our anger simply and straightforwardly, without condemning those we love and making them feel guilty.

We can learn to share our joy. We are created with a sense of joy about living. If we bottle up our joy, we learn a pattern of bottling up. If we bottle something up, we tend to bottle everything up. We bottle up the feeling of joy and we start to bottle up everything, including our excitement, our laughter, and we begin to bottle up our anger, our resentment, our guilt, and anxieties as well. Likewise, as we bottle up our fears and anxieties, we bottle up our sense of joy.

If we learn how to express some of our feelings, we tend to learn how to express more of our feelings. We can learn how to express our joy, our humor, and our laughter. We can learn how to share our feelings of good fun and good times. As we learn how to express these positive feelings, we also learn how to express our feelings of anxiety, anger, resentment, guilt, and bitterness constructively. As we discover ways we can share joy and compassion, laughter and good fun, we also learn the capacity to make amends. Likewise, as we learn how to share our feelings of anger and fear constructively, we discover richer, fuller ways to share a sense of joy in living.

Jesus describes the Kingdom of God as a wedding feast, as a great banquet. This life is a wedding feast of joy, a great banquet of grace. As we experience the grace of God, we learn the capacity to share our feelings helpfully. When we return to the dock, our lives have about them a sense of profound joy.

Living in and Trusting God

In the small, seaport town on the northern coast of Africa there was much excitement: a ship had been sighted early that morning on the horizon. Hippo was a Roman town, an outpost of the empire. You could tell that by its white gleaming buildings, its forum, and its harbor. The ship would bring family, visitors, goods, and news of what was happening across the empire. But there was concern. Shadows had been gathering across the empire.

Late that afternoon, three good friends gathered for an early supper in the refectory next to the church. They could tell by the clamor of the crowd that the ship had landed. The news seemed of a wailing nature, not good, more than tragic, rushing up the hillside in lamenting moans and agonizing screams.

A messenger ran as swiftly as he could up the hill to the refectory. He burst through the door, shouting as though all of his dearest friends and family had died. "Rome is fallen. Alaric and the barbarians have burned and sacked the eternal city." That awful, calamitous event in A.D. 410 brought with it the eventual collapse of the Roman Empire, of civilization in that time.

Marcellinus, the Roman tribune of Hippo, is understood to have said, "If Rome has fallen, Hippo will be not far behind." His words were prophetic. Twenty years later, in A.D. 430, Hippo was sacked and put to dust by the barbarians.

Aelyppius, the bishop of nearby Tegast, is understood to have said, "They will blame the Christians." And they did. This explains the outbreak of persecutions in the empire following the fall of Rome. They did blame the Christians.

The emperor Constantine had begun the process of recognizing Christianity, among the legitimate religions of the empire, with his victory at the battle of the Milvian Bridge in A.D. 312. This culminated in the extraordinary Council of Nicaea in A.D. 325, where, though yet unbaptized but as the Emperor, Constantine presided over the creedal debates. Eighty-five short years after that great council, Rome, the eternal city, was sacked and burned.

Rome had been doing well before this Christian God came on the scene. The older gods had done well by the empire. So it must be the Christian God's fault.

Augustine, the Bishop of Hippo, is understood to have spoken last among the three: "We have loved Rome too much. All civilizations rise and fall. All empires come and go. The city of God is eternal."

Rome is eternal. The phrase had been repeated for centuries. It was the glue of civilization from time immemorial, back beyond almost anyone's memory. It was the phrase that the Roman legions thought of as they marched into battle, that shopkeepers knew would sustain their businesses, that families counted on in their living and dying. Rome is eternal.

Augustine took that ancient phrase and, in an effort to make some sense of life following the collapse of Rome, declared with a newfound sense of living in and trusting God, "The city of God is eternal."

We can learn much from that fateful time. My good friends, all civilizations rise and fall, come and go. All institutions rise and fall, come and go. For Augustine, the appropriate declaration of that time was, "The city of God is eternal." In our time, the helpful way forward is to confirm that *the mission of God is eternal.* We can live in and trust God, with the confidence that the mission of God is eternal.

In Isaiah 40:8, we discover these words: "The grass withers, the flower fades; but the word of God will stand for ever." In our time, the words have this meaning: "The grass withers, the flower fades, but the mission of God shall stand forever." With this confidence, we can live in and trust God.

In our time, institutions come and go. Nations rise and fall. The human hurts and hopes of persons all around us cry out for help, hope, and home. These are urgent, desperate times. These times invite our deepest compassion. We will have experiences of sorrow, despair, depression, and despondency. It comes with the terrain. We can live in and trust God. Sorrow invites joy. Despair invites mission. Depression invites compassion. The way forward beyond despondency is hope. The joy of the Lord is our strength.

God has given us a new day. This is not a time for sorrow. This is an Easter time. Just when some of us have thought that life was about half over, and all we had to do was stay out of major trouble until the end, our God gives us a new day. We want our lives to count. We want our lives to be more than a pleasant merry-go-round that goes nowhere, where the music is charming, the company congenial, and the activities busy, cheery, and sociable.

Now, God invites us to a mission field. Our lives count in an extraordinary way. It is not always pleasant. Life is complex, ambiguous, tenuous. There are occasions when we feel more battle fatigued, bleary eyed, and burned out than ever before. There are times when we draw deeply on our own best creativity, strongest competencies, and deepest compassion.

We live with a sense of wonder about life and the mission God gives us. We learn how to relax and have fun amidst the tensions of the times. We develop our ability to express our feelings constructively and helpfully. We live in and trust God. We live in joy.

--------o--------

Lord God, help us share joy and thankfulness
     with those around us.
          Help us share appreciation and compassion.
When we are anxious, help us share our anxiety
     without blaming those around us.
When we are fearful, help us share our fears
     without frightening those we love.
When we are angry, help us share our anger
     in simple ways, without condemning those
          we love and making them feel guilty.
Help us share in the joy of the Lord, this day and forevermore.
Amen.

10

WISDOM

DR. POLITELLA WAS A GIFTED TEACHER. I can see him now. Thin body, small of stature, slightly bent forward at the shoulders, hands clasped in front, he relished each new idea as a radiant discovery and taught us the wisdom of the ages. His voice was soft, almost hushed. It was as though he were bowing with humility before the truth, reverently, quietly sharing. The class leaned forward to catch each precious, thoughtful word, to hear the wisdom his almost whispery voice shared. His enthusiasm for discernment, for insight, for meaning in life drew the class to new discoveries.

He had a gentle manner. His dark hair was combed back, lying flat. His glasses were perched forward on his nose, almost ready to fall off. He always wore a dark suit, with a subtle tie neatly in place. His tender smile was like the gentle dawning of a new day, the miracle of wisdom in his face. That is how I remember Dr. Politella.

He radiated wisdom. His way of teaching was sacramental in spirit, an outward, visible sign of the inner, spiritual gift of wisdom. The joy of discovery, the wonder of a new idea, the gift of a new insight, he was all of these. He was my professor for my philosophy major, and the most revered, respected professor in the university.

He loved to share the history of ideas: Plato, Aristotle, and the philosophers of the ages, come and gone. Eastern philosophy, historical philosophy, contemporary philosophy, logic, ethics, the range of subjects in which he was deeply conversant was remarkable.

Mostly, he shared wisdom. He helped us think and encouraged us to discover wisdom, think deeply and fully, see in the obvious the deeper meanings of life, look beyond the apparent. He taught us meekness before the truth. He taught us judgment, vision, common sense.

In the intervening years, I have had the privilege of knowing, working with, and sharing with many persons who have known something of

wisdom. Some have been noted theologians. Some have been dishwash-
ers. Some have raised families. Some have built solid businesses. Some
have found wisdom in hard ways, walking through many valleys of the
shadow. Some have come upon wisdom gently enough, as though, on a
pleasant, not-too-warm day, they discovered a good friend in wisdom.

Meekness

One key, one possibility, for a whole, healthy life is wisdom. God invites
us to a life of wisdom, not confusion. We grow forward in life when,
amidst the confusions, chaos, and competing claims that abound, we discover the resources for wisdom in our lives by developing:

- A sense of meekness before the truth
- The benefit of helpful mentors
- A sense of vision for my life
- Common sense in living life

God invites us to a life of wisdom. We are at our best when, amidst the
perplexities and puzzles around us, we discover the resources for a life of
wisdom.

One resource for wisdom is meekness: quiet willingness to be open to
the truth. We are invited to have a gentle, unobstructing spirit, to not let
one's ego get in the way, to be kind toward the truth. We are encouraged
to be open and receptive, ready to yield to new insights and new discoveries. People with a sense of meekness know what they do not know. They
have an abiding gratitude and modesty for what they have learned. Their
experience is that the more they know, the more they discover what they
do not know.

Meekness is the beginning of wisdom. Ultimately, I think only the meek
are really wise. Matthew 5:5 teaches us these words of Jesus: "Blessed are
the meek, for they shall inherit the earth." In Matthew 11:29 (KJV), Jesus
says, ". . . I am meek and lowly in heart. . . ."

Meekness is not low self-esteem masquerading as a virtue. It is not the
plaintive, whining plea, "I don't know." Meekness is not ignorance, nor
is it a tamely docility, a servile submissiveness. Meekness is an abiding,
strong sense that there are more wonders to discover, more of wisdom to
discern, than stars we have found in the sky.

People who develop a know-it-all attitude are overcompensating for low
self-esteem. They imagine, by showing off what they know, that they are
able to cover their own sense of low self-esteem. Sometimes, they practice

intellectual intimidation. They cite this obscure authority or that remote work. Their intricate sentences, fancy words, and erudite sayings are intended to keep others from noticing their own lack of self-confidence.

Wisdom begins with meekness. On occasion, persons with a know-it-all attitude are simply in the very beginning stages of learning. They have discovered just enough of the richness of wisdom to allow their enthusiasm to flourish. They have yet to discover enough in the realm of wisdom to learn how much there is to discover further. So long as they do not become fixated in that early stage, they grow forward. Meekness helps.

It impresses me that genuine experts in any field have both a quiet confidence, a steady, unassuming assurance for what they do know, and a deep, abiding meekness for what they have yet to learn. Wisdom lacks arrogance. Wisdom is not pompous. Wisdom does not boast. The beginning of wisdom is meekness.

Helpful Mentors

A second resource for wisdom is the benefit of helpful mentors in our lives. Wisdom is not simply of our own doing. God helps us discover our mentors, that we might learn well from them. They are the trusted counselors and guides who enrich our lives. They stir our interest in wisdom. They are gracious to share their wisdom and experience with us. Most important, they give us a quest for wisdom and the desire for discovery.

Some of our mentors have been helpful to us in the past. We have not seen them for years, and yet they are with us still. We sense their presence with us. Their wisdom and experience continue to guide us. Some of our mentors are with us now. Wisdom comes as we sense the presence of our mentors with us.

In the early evening, the group gathered for the celebration. As I remember, there were about sixty people there, of various ages and from many walks of life. The number of very young persons was remarkable, and there were many seasoned, older persons as well. It was an open meeting of Alcoholics Anonymous, so a number of us had come as guests for this special occasion. The group was celebrating the "birthdays" of its members. There was warmth and excitement in the air. People shared happy, close greetings with one another. Several brought refreshments for after the meeting.

The group moved quickly through the preliminaries of the meeting. They wanted to get those done. They had come to celebrate special birthdays. They began by honoring those who were celebrating their first birthday—their first year of sobriety. Three persons were. There was

applause and laughter, deeply felt support and enthusiasm as they shared
their stories. The group leader moved on to ask for persons who were
celebrating their second birthday. One person was. He shared his experience. We then honored, in turn, persons who were celebrating their
third, fourth, fifth, sixth birthdays, and so forth. We came to the moment,
for which all of us were waiting, when the group leader said, "Do we
have someone who is celebrating his or her twelfth birthday tonight?"

Mary stood, with a radiance, confidence, and assurance on her face,
and said, "Hi, I'm Mary. I'm an alcoholic." The group responded, warmly
and affectionately, "Hi, Mary."

Mary went on to say she was celebrating her twelfth birthday in the
program. She shared her wisdom and experience with the group. She
recounted some of the difficult times in her pilgrimage. She shared her
growth in the Twelve Step program. Mostly, she thanked her sponsor for
being with her in her journey. She wanted the group to know how much
her sponsor meant to her, and how much wisdom and experience she had
gained from her sponsor. As she spoke, there were moments of lively
enthusiasm and clapping, murmured understanding, some tears, and
deeply felt joy. When her sponsor gave Mary her twelve-year chip, the
group stood, cheering and applauding, sharing its full love and appreciation for this major birthday in Mary's life.

That night, as I listened to Mary share her appreciation for her sponsor and mentor, my mind was stirred to remember all the mentors who
have meant much to me in my own life. I remembered Dr. Joseph Politella.
The picture of him mentoring me came clearly to my mind. Remember-
ing Dr. Politella, I then recalled many of the other mentors who have
enriched my life. My parents, my grandparents, Julie's parents (Alger and
Marion McCoy), her brother Gene, Maurine Pershing, Calvin Heintz,
Harriet Piggott, Ida Mae Stratton, Orville and Mary Hissom, Harold and
Wilma Dodds, Tony Lomelo, Dr. David Shipley, Tom and Dee Shipp,
Olive Smith, Dr. John Deschner, Dr. Marvin and Murlene Judy, Merle and
Roberta Weaver, Gene and Ann St. Clair, Glen and Virginia Johnson, Dr.
Eugene Bianchi, Dr. Earl and Ethel Brewer . . . the list goes on and on of
the persons who have been rich, full mentors with me.

One helpful way you can deepen your life is to remember your mentors, and how their wisdom and experience have helped you grow and
develop. Treat yourself the way your helpful mentors have treated you,
and you treat yourself constructively and healthfully. Relate to persons
around you the way your helpful mentors have related to you, and you
grow the health and wholeness of your life.

You can advance and strengthen your life by selecting some person or persons to serve as your mentor now. Your mentor, just as in your past, helps you grow you. Look for a person like the mentors who have meant much to you. Look for a person who has gifts matching the specific keys among the twelve keys you are seeking to grow forward. Your relationship with your mentor can be both intentional and informal. The primary purpose is mentoring, coaching, encouraging.

Gather with your mentor as often as helps you, but not so often that you start getting more help than is helpful. The art of your mentor is to deliver almost enough help to be helpful, but not so much help that the help is harmful. Share with your mentor the possibilities, among the twelve keys, you plan to grow forward. Your mentor can share with you wisdom, experience, and encouragement. Surrounded by the presence of the mentors of your past and your current mentor in the present, you have major resources for your life. Wisdom comes.

God comes to us directly. God comes to us in Jesus Christ. God comes to us in the Spirit. God comes to us in our mentors. God helps us discover wise mentors to help us grow forward in this life. Our lives have a sense of confidence and assurance, a deep, abiding resource for living as we sense the presence of our mentors with us. Our lives benefit from the mentors who have helped us in the past and who are helping us now.

Hebrews 12:1 shares these words: "Therefore since we are surrounded by so great a cloud of witnesses. . . ." Picture a stadium full of witnesses. The witnesses are our mentors, encouragers, coaches, the people who encourage us, cheer us on, who wish for us the best, and who help us live life at our best.

When we sense the presence of our mentors with us, our lives have a sense of presence and assurance. We are more at peace. We draw on their wisdom. We have a sense of confidence. We know we are not alone. We know there are people who love us, care for us, encourage us, want for us the best in this life and in the next. The benefit of helpful mentors enriches our lives. With our mentors, wisdom comes.

Vision

A third resource for wisdom is vision. We lead healthy lives as we have a sense of vision for our lives. Vision is about more than a misplaced preoccupation as to whether we are going to survive or not. If we reduce our vision for our lives to our survival, we do not even survive. We are already dead.

Many of you who know me well know that I do not say much, in my teachings or in my writings, about vision. Some of you have remarked on this from time to time, noting that many writers have almost an excessive preoccupation with the concept of vision. As I reflect on this, it comes to me that my reticence does not have to do with vision. It has to do with this: so many of the so-called vision statements boil down to a statement calling for the institutional survival of some organization. Vision has to do with life, not institutionalism.

Say to yourself, "I have this vision for my life." Then go on to describe the sense of vision you see as important for your life. We do want our lives to count. We do want to lead lives of value, purpose, and significance. We do want to make some difference. Our sense of vision helps us do so.

Vision is rooted in what counts in the end. Vision is more than idealism. There are two intriguing problems with idealism. The first is that idealism gets so caught up in itself that it cannot distinguish between the consequential and the inconsequential, the 20 percenters and the 80 percenters. Idealism, regrettably, becomes so smitten with itself—idealism for the sake of idealism—that it can no longer make wise judgments as to what really counts. Instead, everything alleges to be important.

The second problem is this: idealism is the ancestor of cynicism. People who head for the idealism eventually become disappointed. Depression and despair set in. The pendulum swings, and the idealists head for cynicism. Their lofty idealism, their preoccupation with everything as though all things are of equal weight and value, leads to disappointments, despair, and depression. Cynicism enters.

The antidote to idealism is vision: vision that has about it a sense of wisdom and judgment. Martin Luther King Jr. expressed his vision for his life and mission in his speech, "I Have a Dream." Vision recognizes that some things, not all things, are of value in this life. What counts has to do with human hurts and people's hopes. Vision helps us discern what is genuinely important in our lives.

Common Sense

A fourth resource for wisdom is common sense. Wisdom is not grandiose and flamboyant. Wisdom is down to earth. God invites us to use our best common sense. Wisdom and common sense are good friends. We are encouraged to value and exercise common sense in our lives. Wisdom is not simply found in data and detail, however helpful they may be. Sometimes the more data and detail we have, the more confused we become. We lose sight of the day-to-day possibilities and realities of life. Data, by itself, does not help us discern the wise way forward. Wisdom is found in common sense.

Someone once said, "If common sense were that common, more people would have it." I do think common sense is common. Many people simply do not consciously draw forward what, in fact, they intuitively know. Thousands of times, people have come to me at the close of a seminar and said things like, "Thank you. What you have shared makes sense. As we listened, we realized we knew what you were teaching us. We simply didn't know we knew." Or, "As you were talking, it dawned on me that I knew what you were sharing. I just didn't realize I did." Or, "I appreciate your helping us discover what we knew—and now know we knew."

Given half a chance, most people have the capacity for common sense. Whenever we are too tense and tight, too nervous and anxious, too caught up in busyness, we lose sight of our common sense.

Much of life is common sense. We have a spirit of integrity about who we are and what we are about. We do not bemoan past mistakes. They are the dust of antiquity. We learn from them. We move on. We focus on what is really consequential, the 20 percenters. Common sense helps us discover what really counts in life, and as we so do we find meaning and purpose in our lives.

Sometimes, even if we do discern the consequential, nevertheless we allow ourselves to be drawn to the inconsequential. What frequently happens is that we look for activities with quick closure, immediate satisfaction, short-term results. One of the "Star Trek" episodes was about "the trouble with tribbles." Tribbles were warm, fuzzy, furry creatures that did absolutely nothing except eat voraciously and multiply rapidly. They multiplied so rapidly that they began to take up all the space aboard the ship and to weigh the ship down so much that it could barely fly.

This is what many of the activities in life do to us. They take up too much space and time in our lives and weigh us down too much. Such activities create busyness, frustration, and a hectic schedule. We feel we are rushing hither and yon, with a frantic pace and the sense that we are not, in the long run, investing our time and our life constructively. The art of dealing with such activities is twofold. First, with common sense, discern what is really important and consequential in your life and invest your best energies and creativity in it.

Second, with common sense, discern what is not consequential and invest only modest energy in it. The mistake would be to invest our best energies and creativity in activities that in the end are not consequential. Yes, we do inconsequential things in this life. When they come to us, we do them with honor, integrity, and competency. We know they deliver only modest results. We are at peace as we do them. We do not allow ourselves to get caught up in them. We do not unwisely try to make them into consequential matters.

Years ago, and even now, I wrestle with how best to invest the time God gives me. I am wise enough to know that one cannot avoid taking care of some matters that are ultimately not consequential. Indeed, although they have only modest value, they are in their own right worthy of doing well.

Late one night, my mind came to this advance on the 20 percent, 80 percent principle. I call it the Callahan principle of wisdom:

> Investing 20 percent of your time in the 20 percenters yields 80 percent of your results, accomplishments, and achievements.

This principle is a helpful insight toward developing a life of quality. If you invest 80 percent of your time in the 80 percenters, that is fine, too.

We do not need to invest all of our time in the 20 percenters. That is unrealistic. The 20 percenters do not need that much of our time. What helps is for us to invest some of our best, most creative time in those matters that are consequential. This invites our best common sense.

It is difficult to discern what is genuinely important in life. Some people tend to polarize the conversation, to insist that the specific way they see life is the only way. They insist on conformity to their way of thinking. Yet even those who most insist on conformity innately sense that a narrow, rigid perspective, circumspectly constructed and defended, does not last.

What is needed for our lives is a direction, a way forward, not a narrow, tidy solution. What is needed is to help people make sense of life—for this time—in the light of the gospel. Shallow slogans and flimsy conformities will not help us. This is not a time for ignorance or arrogance, foolishness or pretension. Gimmicks and gadgets, tricks and trivialities do not sustain us.

This is the time to gather our best thinking, our thoughtful discernment. This is the time to discover our deepest understanding of life, so that we can make some sense of the time God gives us. This is the time for meekness, mentors, vision, and common sense. With these resources we discover wisdom to help us live our lives wholly and healthfully.

———— o ————

God of grace and of galaxies, of salvation and solar systems,
  we are grateful for Your compassion with us.
The immensity of the universe teaches us the immensity of Your
love for us.
  Stir our strengths. Touch our lives.
The worst of us is in the best of us. The best of us is in the worst
of us.
  Cleanse the worst from within us.
    Forgive our feeble sins. Have mercy on our terrible sins.
Grant us meekness. Give us mentors to help us live well.
  Help us have vision. May common sense walk with us as our
good friend.
    Give us wisdom.
  We pray, trusting in Your grace. Amen.

11

ENCOURAGEMENT

I MET SAM when he was in his early twenties. I always called him Sam. Most people, including his mama, called him Sammy. By the time I met Sam, he had found his way into more trouble and difficulty than most people can figure out how to get into in four lifetimes. The mess he had made of his life was amazing to behold.

In the early years of grade school, Sam came home with Cs and Bs on his report card. His mama would say, "Sammy, you can do better."

Sammy would do better. In junior high school, he came home with a few Bs and mostly As. His mama would say, "Sammy, you can do better."

Sammy would do better. In high school, he came home with all As. He was the star quarterback of the football team, setting new passing and running records. He was All State. He was elected president of the student body. He was voted most popular in the school. His mama would say, "Sammy, you can do better."

He went to a ranking college, started as quarterback of the varsity team in his freshman year, made all As, and was elected president of his class.

At every stage in his life, his mama said, "Sammy, you can do better." Translation: "Sammy, you never do well enough. Sammy, you always fail."

He dropped out of college and bummed around. He didn't do much of anything; then he began to find his way into trouble. He found more trouble than made good sense for someone with his abilities. He was in considerable difficulty.

By the time I met Sam, he had so successfully developed an identity of failure that every time he got near success, he would marshal all of his considerable strengths and competencies to guarantee that he would fail yet another time.

Sharing "Well Done"

One key, one possibility, for a whole, healthy life is encouragement. God invites us to a life of encouragement, not threat and fear. Sharing the grace of encouragement is one of the rare gifts in life. We live constructive lives when, amidst the disappointments and calamities, dread and fright, menace and peril of life that abound, we have the quality of encouragement in our lives by

- ○ Sharing the gift of "well done" with people
- ○ Discovering a life of grace
- ○ Developing a sense of humor
- ○ Living a life of progress

I asked Sam, "Across the years, do you remember anyone who said to you, 'Well done'?" He could faintly remember a third-grade teacher who had been a mentor, friend, wise and caring teacher. There were times when she said, "Well done." But the words Sam heard too frequently from his well-meaning mamma were, "Sammy, you can do better." The message was that he never did "good enough." He always failed.

A first source of encouragement is found in sharing, deeply and appreciatively, "Well done." The words *well done* are like drenching rains in a desert. They are like soothing, cooling breezes on a hot, scorching day. They are words of life and hope.

In the end, the old poem is not helpful:

> Good, better, best,
> never let it rest,
> till your good is better
> and your better is best.

That poem hung for years at the front of classrooms, with the alleged purpose of encouraging students. As a matter of fact, it taught a pattern of failure that has been fatal to many.

We are invited to be encouraging with those around us, even as God is encouraging with us. The primary attribute of God is amazing grace and mercy with us. God creates the universe to help us know the immensity of God's love with us. God encourages us. God sends Jesus to share with us the good news of grace and to encourage us to live a healthy life. God surrounds us with wonder and joy, hope and new life. God is present with us as the Holy Spirit, as the Comforter, as the Spirit of Encouragement, stirring and leading us to that future which God is preparing for us. God encourages you. The words *well done* are words of grace and mercy, encouragement and appreciation. Share with many persons the words "well done."

In the New Testament, I am amazed at the many ways, directly and indirectly, in which Jesus says, "Well done." In the parable of the talents, the lord gives specific talents to his servants, counting on his servants to grow them. Two of the three servants accomplish what they are asked to achieve. The first servant comes back, saying:

> "Lord, you entrusted five talents to me; see, I have gained five more talents." His Lord said to him, "Well done, good and faithful servant; you were faithful with a few things; I will put you in charge of many things. Enter into the joy of your Lord."
>
> The second servant came back, saying, "Lord, you entrusted two talents to me; see, I have gained two more talents." His Lord said to him, "Well done, good and faithful servant; you were faithful with a few things; I will put you in charge of many things. Enter into the joy of your Lord." Matthew 25:20–23

Two of the three servants did excellent work. We have been too preoccupied with the one servant who buried his one talent in the ground to conserve and hold, protect and preserve it. In the parable, two servants advance and build what they were given. To each of these, the lord says, "Well done, thou good and faithful servant." For all of us, two of the most helpful, encouraging words in life are *well done*. God wants for us a strong, healthy life. God gives each of us distinctive talents. God encourages us to develop the talents God gives us. As we do, God says, "Well done."

Sometimes we do a pretty good job of sharing "well done," of sharing with others positive recognition for excellent results. We offer words of appreciation and praise. We share gratitude and recognition. We say "well done" with warmth and affection. Remember the people who have meant the most to you. These are most frequently those who have shared with you, "Well done." Go and do likewise. Go and be like them: with your family, friends, community, and the people with whom you work.

The learning, for many of us, is to do the same with ourselves. We sometimes denigrate our own accomplishments and achievements. We sometimes do not value and appreciate what we have achieved. We look too much at our mistakes and failures and do not learn from them. We become so absorbed in our next project that we do not claim the success of our recent achievements.

Sometimes, we look back too much at the failures that have been. Sometimes we look too much ahead at the things yet to be done. Thus we miss the joy of the accomplishments in the present. We miss the "well done." People who share "well done" have developed their capacity to see the best in persons.

Discovering Grace

A second source of encouragement is to live a life of grace. We can be considerate and thoughtful with those around us. We can share a sense of dignity and honor with them. We can have a disposition toward gratefulness and kindness. We can share unmerited assistance in ways that are helpful. We can share the richness of grace.

Sometimes, we become preoccupied with threat and fear. We spend too much time threatening those around us. In effect, we say, "If you don't do such and such, then this threat is going to happen to you." We try to motivate with fear. Fear is a demotivator, not a motivator. Yes, threats may cause us to do something. Many persons do something out of fear: the fear of failure, loneliness, meaninglessness, hopelessness, punishment, or death.

But whatever its face and focus, fear causes us to become tense, tight, nervous, anxious. We are not our best selves. Some of our best strengths and competencies are frozen, paralyzed. We may, in fact, achieve something—usually less than what we might have accomplished. Frequently, what we achieve when motivated by fear is a strikeout.

Consider what one can do when fear is not present. In sports events, the pros, even coming from behind to achieve an upset, an unheard-of win, are asked what is the secret to their astonishing success. What they talk about is deciding to relax and have fun. They put aside any focus on failure. They decide to have a good time. They win. They talk about setting aside any fear or trepidation. They talk about the grace people have shared with them.

Under threat, people wither. With grace, people grow. Grace is stronger than fear. Fear is strong. Grace is stronger. Grace is stronger than law. Law is strong. Grace is stronger. We can share the rich, full gift of grace.

Sometimes, we become preoccupied with complaining and nitpicking. Some people, over many years, develop a pattern of behavior that is picky and petty. They whine and complain, lament and bemoan this or that. It is too hot; then it is too cold. Friends never visit; they are always too busy. Then, when they do visit, they stay too long.

People with confidence and assurance live a life of grace. People who doubt themselves have difficulty living a life of grace. I asked one wise, caring leader to share her wisdom about people who complain a lot. She said, "It has been my observation that people who complain a lot are unhappy within themselves." I thought about that for some time. A long time later, it came to me. People who complain a lot, who are picky and petty, tend to look down on themselves, to think poorly of themselves. Then they pity their self-imposed, imagined plight in life. Wherever the old nemeses Picky and Petty show up, their quaint friend Pity is not far behind.

Complaining and nitpicking seem to go hand-in-hand. We do not even realize how much we pick. The words spew from our mouths and we almost do not realize we are saying them: "Don't do this." "Not now." "Don't do that." "Keep out of that." "Put that away." "Why can't you ever do anything right?" "Wait till later." "Don't ask why. Just do it." "You've done it wrong again." There is too much nitpicking in this world.

We imagine that the nitpicking we deliver somehow causes people around us to do what is constructive. We go overboard. We try to force people when we could lead people. We share nitpicking when we could share grace. What helps most of us is someone who loves us, who is a sacramental person of grace with us, who accepts us for who we are, not for who they think we should be. People long for grace.

Sometimes we become preoccupied with giving too much advice. Many times, we give too much advice to people around us. When we persist with advice to those around us, we communicate, regrettably, that we do not accept them for who they are, that we only accept them for who we want them to be. We end up spending too much time correcting. We spend too much time on what they are doing wrong, their failures and shortcomings, and thus we do not share grace with them.

What helps most of us are tons of grace, bushels of confidence, mountains of assurance, and, maybe on occasion, a little suggestion or a wee bit of advice. The art is coaching, not correcting; grace, not law. Persons who have some sense of confidence and assurance in themselves share a deep, rich, full spirit of grace, generously and readily.

When someone gives you advice, rather than grace, know three things. First, they likely want to help. They are not trying to do you harm. Their intentions are well meaning. They seek to do good. Second, they learned somewhere the behavior pattern of wanting to give advice. Most likely, they learned it in their own earlier years, from other persons who frequently gave them advice. It is freeing to discover they learned this behavior pattern from someone else and that therefore we need not take too personally the advice giving. They are living out what they learned.

Third, they lack some confidence and self-assurance. They project this lack onto you. They therefore hope the advice they give you will remedy the deficiency. They see you as an extension of themselves and hope to remedy in you the fault they see in themselves. When you are prone to give advice quickly, consider that these same three things may be at work in you.

Grace listens. Advice talks. Grace is humble. Advice is prideful. Grace is gentle. Advice is intrusive. Grace is slow to speak. Advice is quick to answer. Grace knows there are many ways to do something. Advice always knows "the right way" it must be done. Grace sees the best in you. Grace helps.

Have confidence and assurance in yourself. Then you share grace with others. Listen well. Be slow to give advice. Be even slower still to share threats. Be not anxious and fearful. Discover the spirit of grace.

Developing a Sense of Humor

A third source of encouragement is to develop a sense of humor. Live a life of humor, not of tense, tight seriousness. Humor is salve for the soul. Laughter is rain in a barren wasteland. Humor is like drenching rain in a scorching desert. People who live a life of encouragement have developed a sense of humor.

One night, while working on a complex dilemma, these words came to me:

> Blessed are those who can laugh, for they shall enjoy life.
> Blessed are those with a sense of humor, for their lives shall be rich and full.
> Blessed are those who can laugh with others, for they shall never cease to have company.

Sometimes, I think it is equally important to affirm: blessed are those who can laugh at themselves, for they are frequently amused.

In a movement I respect deeply, Alcoholics Anonymous, there is Rule 63. It is said that Rule 63 came about this way. In the early, formative years of AA, Bill W. and Dr. Bob gathered about one hundred of the earliest recovering alcoholics to set forth a charter about who they planned to be as an organization, who could join, what the duties of membership would be, and so forth.

In the meeting, eagerly, compulsively, almost addictively, they conjured up rule upon rule, requirement upon requirement. With considerable detail and precision, they quickly created sixty-two rules and regulations, conditions and stipulations, policies and procedures.

In a moment of wonderful, awesome discovery, they realized what they had done. Their compulsiveness and addictiveness had run rampant in yet another way. They discovered they had almost become addicted to their own recovery, which in itself was unhealthy, simply another form of addiction. Thus, with some good humor, they created Rule 63:

> We will not take ourselves too seriously.

They scrapped the other rules. They decided that whoever wanted to claim to be a member was therefore a member. As serious, as crucial as the work of that movement is, even in the most precarious life-and-death situations, it is freeing to be able to not take oneself too seriously.

Humor helps us not take ourselves too seriously. Humor helps us see the irony of life, see the fading flimsiness of so much that we have created and taken oh-so-seriously. Humor helps us beyond the careful precision with which we try to order life. If we are able to have a sense of humor, if we do not take our own selves too seriously, we are able to share the gift of encouragement with those around us.

A Life of Progress

A fourth source of encouragement is to develop a life of progress. This does not mean that life is always getting better and better. It does mean that, amidst the difficulties and struggles of life, we are moving forward. We have the sense that we are growing a whole, healthy life.

God invites us to a life of progress, not perfectionism. Perhaps some of us learned to drive ourselves toward perfectionism in our growing up years. It is not so much that we intended to learn this pattern. One day we looked around and discovered that this way of living life had crept up on us.

That old friend has been with us much too long. Frequently, we do not even remember from whom we learned to be a perfectionist. Yet, we learned it from someone, or, more likely, from several people. We might have learned it from

- Parents who were simply seeking to be good parents and who likely learned it from their parents, who kept saying, "You can do better"
- A teacher who tried to cause us to strive for our best
- A loved one who saw the best *in* us and wanted, even more, the best *for* us

We might have learned the pattern as our way to overcompensate for our own low self-esteem. Or we might have learned the pattern out of a desire to do well. This became our understanding of how to be helpful.

A *compulsiveness toward perfectionism* causes us to set too many objectives too high to be accomplished too soon. This causes us to postpone action. We postpone action in order to postpone failure. Innately, we know we have set ourselves up to fail. We postpone action in order to postpone failure.

Procrastination is the symptom, not the cause. Some of us spend half our lives kicking ourselves for procrastination, for delaying, for putting off. The real problem is not procrastination. It is perfectionism. We procrastinate to postpone failure.

If we postpone action, it leads to depression. Depression is anger turned within. We are angry with ourselves that we have once again set ourselves up to fail. We have been down this dark hole before. We are angry that, once again, we have allowed the old pattern of perfectionism to overtake us. And that sense of depression leads to dependency. We now look for a codependent relationship to assuage our depression.

There are two old friends. Wherever a compulsiveness toward perfectionism is found, there also is the old friend of *a pervasive sense of powerlessness*. Perfectionism yields depression and dependency. These create a feeling, an attitude, a foreboding. A sense of powerlessness follows. We feel we can do nothing to advance our situation. We feel powerless. Thus, we set no goals to be achieved, not ever, and we nurture low self-esteem. This results in inaction. Inaction leads to further depression and deeper dependency.

A third old friend joins in: *a state of wishful thinking*. The deeper the sense of powerlessness, the deeper the depression and dependency. As the depression deepens and the dependency flourishes, we are then more likely to head for a state of wishful thinking. Wishful thinking entices us to chase unrealistic generalities and vague fantasies. We imagine that if only something miraculous happens, we will be, immediately, now, this minute, all right.

We become addicted to wishful thinking. We concoct all sorts of schemes and dreams to leap from the misery of the moment to an instantaneous, bright, new future. Mostly, in the way we imagine it, these schemes do not depend on us. They depend on some outside person or group doing something for us. This in itself is a form of dependency. We look outside ourselves for the solution to our predicament rather than looking inside ourselves for new sources of health and wholeness. The depression deepens. The dependency grows.

A fourth old friend comes on board: *an excessive drive toward achievement.* The more persistent the state of wishful thinking, the more excessive and determined the drive toward achievement. If a state of wishful thinking overcomes us, there ensues a determined drive toward achievement. We set too many objectives, too high, to be accomplished too soon. Moreover, tragically, now we have no patience with ourselves, let alone with those around us.

This leads to excessive action and high frustration. We engage in a flurry of activity, working harder and harder. We become more determined and dogged. We put in longer hours; become tenser and tighter; nervous and anxious. We take out our high frustration on ourselves and on everyone around us. This pattern leads to failure and, thereby, deeper depression and richer dependency. Now, we really look for a codependent relationship. We wallow in our misery.

I have described these four patterns sequentially, because this is the only way I can share them. They often happen sequentially. But sometimes, we become fixated at one point. Frequently, they happen almost simultaneously in us.

Sometime during the coming week, drive out near the middle of nowhere. Not the middle of nowhere, because that is somewhere. If it were somewhere, others might find the place. Near the middle of nowhere. Have a last farewell conversation with that old friend, a compulsiveness toward perfectionism. Open the car door briskly, shove gently and firmly, close quickly, and drive swiftly down the road. Get that old friend out of your life.

Oh—before you drive down the road, open the back door of your car. Have a last, hurried, fond, farewell conversation with powerlessness, wishful thinking, and an excessive drive toward achievement, shove gently and firmly, close quickly, and head swiftly down the road. Get all four of those old friends out of your life.

A little ways down the road, a new, helpful friend, smiling and encouraging, is standing by the side of the road, hoping you will pull over and welcome this new friend into your life. This new, good friend is progress.

Now, I know it is not as simple as driving out near the middle of nowhere and having that last farewell conversation. Old ways die hard. At the same time, begin now to leave behind those old friends. They have had their day. The former things have passed away. We do learn new ways in Christ.

God invites us to a life of progress, not perfection. Put the three words "progress, not perfection" somewhere where you will see them frequently. Begin your day with the prayer, "God, help me, this one day, to live a life of progress, not perfection."

At lunch, when you say grace, thank God that this morning you have lived a morning of progress. Ask God that this afternoon, as the day continues on, progress, not perfection, will be present with you. At dinner, give thanks to God that this day you have lived in a spirit of progress, not perfectionism. When you go to bed, give thanks to God for this one day of progress. Rest well, knowing it has been a good day.

Progress is one day at a time. Progress is not bigger and better. Our new, good friend, progress helps us

○ Set a few objectives

○ Make them realistic and achievable

○ Have solid time horizons

○ Match with our strengths and competencies

With a few objectives that we can achieve, we head for the action. There is no inaction, no procrastination. With solid action, we accomplish our objectives. There is a sense of satisfaction. With that satisfaction there is a sense of growing and developing in one's life pilgrimage.

Gone is the clamoring and chaos of too many objectives, the cacophony of their being set too high, the commotion and furor of trying to accomplish them too soon. Gone is the pervasive sense of powerlessness, with its despair and defeatism. Gone is the state of wishful thinking, with its tumult and turmoil. Gone is an excessive drive toward achievement, with its rushing, impatient fury and its frantic frenzy of excessive action and high frustration. All these are gone.

People who live a life of progress also live a life of peace. Words I find helpful and frequently share are "Be at peace." They are calming, gentle words. They are like a gentle breeze that takes away the heat of the day.

They are among the most calming, soothing words in the whole of this life's pilgrimage. They bring a stillness and quiet that is sacramental. "Be at peace." These words are not a command. They are a gift. It is not accidental that in gatherings of Christians there is the important sacramental act of passing the peace.

This life is fraught with uncertainty. Sometimes life feels precarious. We develop careful, meticulous customs, habits, traditions, social conformities and conventions, all designed to eliminate the uncertainty of life. But they only create the illusion of certainty.

Serenity is not found in certainty. Peace and serenity are found in a life of progress. Serenity is being at peace about uncertainty, having some confidence and assurance that all is well, that all is in God's gracious, encouraging hands, that what we can do is live a life of progress, each day. God invites us to live lives of peace and serenity. Jesus said, "My peace I give unto you (John 14:27)."

People who live a life of progress also live a life of pace. For some of us, our pace is that of an excellent sprinter. For some, our pace is that of a solid marathon runner. Pace is not a matter of slowing down. It is not a matter of excellent sprinters somehow turning into solid marathon runners and solid marathon runners turning into yet slower marathon runners. Pace is not a matter of speed. It is a matter of selection.

Pace means that the excellent sprinter selects wisely the few sprints, the few objectives, he or she plans to achieve, running as fast as ever but running fewer sprints. The solid marathon runner, who has a sense of pace, selects more wisely the few marathons he or she plans to run. There are fewer objectives, well run, well done.

Those who live a life of progress also live a life of power. There is the quiet power of a few objectives, the silent confidence they are realistic and achievable, the calm certainty that they have solid time horizons. There is the untroubled, hushed movement to action.

As we grow a life of encouragement—sharing the gift of "well done," living a life of grace, having a sense of humor, and living a life of progress—we develop whole, healthy lives. In Luke 6:36 it says, "Be ye therefore merciful, as your Father also is merciful."

The primary attribute of God is amazing grace and mercy with us. We are harder on ourselves than God is on us. God has mercy with us. We can have mercy with ourselves. We can live a life of encouragement.

———— o ————

God of grace and encouragement,
   we are grateful for Your words of "well done."
We are humbly thankful You see the best in us.
   The gift of Your grace is amazing to us. We thank You.
We thank You for the gift of laughter and humor.
   We are better able to live this life through with these good gifts.
Grant us a life of progress and peace.
   Help us not be fearful and anxious.
Give us confidence and assurance that Your grace and love,
   Your peace and serenity surround us and sustain us.
   Amen.

12

CREATIVITY

ON OUR FIRST TRIP to the Bahamas, we left Florida early in the evening, sailing a remarkable thirty-five-foot boat. It would sleep six persons and included a full galley, shower, and head. The mainsail and genoa provided an extraordinary spread of sail. Our destination was Bimini, the nearest landfall to Florida across the Gulf Stream. We had learned from various people who had made the crossing the best way was to sail all night long, arriving early in the morning at Bimini.

The entrance to the harbor is long and narrow. It turns frequently. There are coral reefs and sandbars, creating a twisting, winding course. The challenge is to weave your way among the reefs to the harbor. If you leave Florida in the morning, you get there at nighttime and have to anchor offshore until the next morning. By arriving early in the morning, a person standing on the bow can see the reefs. The water is so clear, you can see almost forever. With these sightings from the bow, you can navigate between the reefs.

I can still see my parents standing on the dock and waving goodbye to their two grandsons, as Julie and I and our two sons left Florida. My parents were convinced, given that we were sailing through what is known as the Bermuda Triangle, this could be the last time they might see their grandsons alive.

During the crossing that night, we had some of the best sailing I've known in my life. I remember around two or two-thirty in the morning, everybody was asleep below. The seas were gentle and rolling. The wind was strong, but not too much. We were making good time. I was at the tiller sailing toward a cluster of stars—not one star, a cluster. It was some of the most incredible sailing I have ever known.

Early that morning, we sighted Bimini. We had stayed the course well. We saw a freighter just off Bimini near the channel. Freighters need deep water. We concluded that if we stayed near the freighter, we would be in deep water and would miss the coral reefs. We stayed steady, moving closer, yet closer to the freighter.

There was a grinding crunch.

One never quite forgets the crunch of the keel of a sailboat on a coral reef. We ran aground near the center of the reef. We soon found out that three days before, the captain of the freighter, who had been sailing twenty-plus years in the Bahamas, had run his freighter onto the center of the coral reef. The closer we got to the freighter, the closer we got to the coral reef.

Our sailboat was now listing dangerously to starboard; then abruptly to port. Back and forth. With the help of a native fisherman and his fishing boat, we got our sailboat off the reef with no damage done—remarkable in that respect. We found our way safely into the Bimini harbor, made our way to a berth and began to calm down after the tension of hitting a coral reef.

We learned that there is a saying in the Bahamas, where there are lots of reefs and shallow water: "If a skipper says he has never run aground, his boat has never left the dock."

The Capacity to Learn from One's Mistakes

One key, one possibility, for a whole, healthy life is creativity. God invites us to a life of creativity, not a routine, habituated life, dull and sluggish, tediously the same. Creativity is a wonderful resource, and you can nurture it by developing

○ Your capacity to learn from your mistakes

○ Your capacity to learn from your achievements

○ Your spirit of flexibility

○ Your capacity to learn in a rich variety of ways

One resource for creativity is the capacity to learn from our mistakes. We make mistakes. Likely, we make more mistakes than we ever imagined or wanted to. Some are minor, incidental ones. Some mistakes are major, grievous ones. It is one thing to confess our mistakes. It is another thing to learn from them. Confession is most helpful. Learning from our mistakes is most helpful. There is little point in continuing to repeat the same mistakes.

We can learn from the minor, incidental mistakes that are part of daily living. We try something simple. It does not work. We try something else.

That doesn't work. Finally, we discover some way forward that works. With minor, incidental activities, we are able to nurture our capacity to learn from our mistakes.

Some mistakes are major, grievous mistakes. They are harmful to the ones we love, to the people around us, and frequently to ourselves. They are the troubling, damaging mistakes, disturbing and injurious. The memory of them is sometimes more than we can bear. We are overcome with the damage these mistakes have done. We wish they had never happened.

These mistakes I refer to as "excellent mistakes." They are really good mistakes. Now, I do not mean to discount the serious damage that these mistakes cause. Rather, I use the term *excellent mistakes* to confirm that they are among the best mistakes we have made. They are major mistakes.

Creativity includes the capacity to learn from our mistakes. We learn from the minor mistakes we make, and most especially we learn from the excellent mistakes, the major mistakes. The more positive the recognition for excellent mistakes, the higher the level of creativity in one's life. Positive recognition means that we acknowledge the mistake and we learn from it. Positive recognition does not mean praising or condoning the mistake that is made. Rather, it means owning up to the mistake, asking for forgiveness, and especially learning from the mistake. It is one thing to confess our mistakes. It is another thing to learn from them. It is an excellent mistake when we learn well from it.

The more negative the recognition of excellent mistakes, the lower the level of creativity in one's life. Negative recognition of mistakes causes people to try never to make a mistake. Further, negative recognition causes them, when they do make a serious mistake, to seek to repress the mistake. They thereby become frozen in the mistake and do not learn from it.

The art is to learn from our mistakes, rather than become frozen by them. When we allow ourselves to make a mistake, we allow ourselves to be creative. It is not that we purposely try to make mistakes, but when we do not allow ourselves to make a mistake, we do not allow ourselves to be creative. The art is to sail forward, not to freeze at the dock. Ships are meant for sailing, not staying at the dock. We are meant for living, not being frozen, fearful and frightened, never leaving the dock.

The creative inventors of our time, and of all previous times, developed the capacity to learn from their mistakes. Indeed, it is only after countless experiments—what I call excellent mistakes—that they come to their discoveries. You will note that I said they *developed the capacity to learn* from their mistakes. The capacity to learn from one's mistakes is a learned behavior pattern.

Some people learn they should never make a mistake. Regrettably, well-intentioned persons taught them this behavior pattern. Whatever they do, they must never *be* a mistake. When people are told frequently enough to never make a mistake, they sometimes conclude, if they ever make one, that they are the mistake. Making a mistake and being a mistake become one and the same. To make a mistake is to be a mistake.

Well-meaning persons whose message to others is to never make a mistake think they are teaching a behavior pattern of excellence. But the lesson people learn is to never make a mistake. The best way to never make a mistake is to never try anything. Creativity is lost.

Such people learn a pattern of thinking, regrettably, that they always make mistakes. Whatever they do, it is always wrong. Unfortunately, some people taught them they always fail, fall short, and make mistakes. The simplest way to never make a mistake is to never do anything. They become frozen at the dock. Creativity is lost.

The beginning of creativity is learning the capacity to learn from one's mistakes. As we remember the mistakes of the past and present, it does not help to denigrate oneself, to punish oneself, to look down on oneself, or to develop doubt about oneself. The art is to value what we learn from our mistakes. When we learn and grow from our mistakes, we encourage our best creativity.

When we deliver positive recognition for excellent mistakes, when we help people learn and grow from their excellent mistakes, we encourage their best spirit of creativity. When we deliver negative recognition for mistakes, when we press people to never make a mistake, we teach them that the best way to never make a mistake is for their boat to never leave the dock. Ships are meant for sailing, not for docking.

The Capacity to Learn from One's Achievements

I was helping a group of people. We were discussing the ways people build strong, healthy lives. I suggested that first we focus on our strengths, gifts, and competencies. We claim them, expand some of them, and add new strengths. Then we are in the best position to deal with our weaknesses and shortcomings.

When we start with our strengths, with a spirit of gratefulness and humility, we develop a life of grace. When we start with our weaknesses, we end up with a life of law, which does not help us discover our strengths. I encouraged the group to put aside that old way of doing things—that we not begin with a long list of weaknesses and mistakes. It simply results in a long list of don'ts and do's, rules and regulations. We begin with our strengths.

An ophthalmologist was in the group. The light dawned. You could see it on his face, in his eyes, hear it in the enthusiasm in his voice.

He observed, somewhat wryly, that he would be a very wealthy person if he had a quarter for each time this happened: he would prescribe new glasses, two to three weeks would pass, and the patient would come back lamenting that the new glasses weren't working. He said, "I would be a very wealthy person if I had a quarter for every time I said, 'Put your old glasses in the drawer. Leave them there. Use your new glasses. Keep your new glasses on.'"

People would leave from their earlier appointment with their new glasses, pleased, happy, seeing better than before. In the weeks that ensued, they would sometimes wear their new glasses, sometimes wear their old glasses, back and forth, back and forth. Their eyes would never adjust to and benefit fully from the new glasses.

He smiled and said to the group that day, "I'm putting my old glasses in the drawer. I'm leaving them there. From this moment on, I will look at life with new glasses."

Begin with your strengths. With new glasses, with a new perspective on your strengths, be open to discovering how you can grow yourself. Your options to expand a current strength and to add a new strength are plentiful.

Your creativity advances as you learn from your strengths and achievements. When you do something that has excellent results, ask yourself, "What can I learn from this?" Discover more fully why it went well. We can become so preoccupied with failures and mistakes that we hardly ever learn from what went well. You can. And you can parallel these learnings into new possibilities. As you nurture your learnings and appreciation for what in fact you have accomplished, and what you are now accomplishing, you grow your confidence to trust in your own creativity.

A Spirit of Flexibility

A third resource for creativity is to grow forward a spirit of flexibility, not rigidity. You can do this as you practice what I call the "two-for-one principle."

I was helping a congregation. Gene and I were visiting on my first day there, in the afternoon. The sunlight was streaming through the windows, on one of those remarkably beautiful days we cherish in life. Gene was one of the central leaders in the church. He and his carpentry team built the original sanctuary, now used as their chapel. Next, he and his construction company built the Christian education building. Importantly, he and his building firm then went on to build the new sanctuary, one of the finest in the region.

The congregation is part of a denomination that historically had not allowed women to vote on congregational matters. Many years before, at the national level of the denomination, the policy had been adopted that women could vote—potentially. It was left to each individual congregation to decide the matter for itself.

Gene said to me, "Dr. Callahan, I see our congregation as an island in the lake." Translation: all the other churches in that denomination in that community had, in recent times, individually decided women could vote on congregational matters. Gene's church had not. In his view, his congregation was upholding the historic tradition of the past.

I said, "Gene, either the island is sinking, or the water is rising, and you and I had better build a bridge to the mainland, or find us a boat, before we are the last ones left on this island as it sinks." We talked long that afternoon.

Bob had come as pastor six years before. He favored women voting. He was considered a liberal. In the late spring at the end of his first year there, he called a congregational meeting to decide whether women could vote. Gene gathered people out of the woodwork to defeat the proposal. Gene won by several votes.

The next year, and for five consecutive years, Bob called for a vote, and each of the five times Gene gathered people out of the woodwork to defeat the proposal. Their liturgical year had become Christmas, Easter, The Vote. The most recent vote happened two weeks before my arrival. There was still lots of heat left.

The second day there, Bob and I were headed to a meeting in his car. I said to Bob, "I have a puzzle. You were here as pastor six months when your secretary said it would be helpful to her if the bulletin could be done on Thursday rather than on Friday. Your response was, 'I have always done the bulletin on Friday, and I don't plan to change now.'

"A couple of years passed. She asked once again about the possibility of the bulletin being done on Thursday rather than Friday. Your response, more firmly and rigidly, was, 'I have always done the bulletin on Friday, and I don't plan to change now.'

"Recently, she and the personnel committee together requested the possibility of the bulletin being done on Thursday rather than Friday. Your entrenched response was, 'I have always done the bulletin on Friday, and I don't plan to change now.'

"You shared much of this with me yesterday.

"Bob, I have this puzzle. On something as simple as the bulletin being done on Thursday or Friday, your response is, 'I have always done the bulletin on Friday, and I don't plan to change now.'

"On something major, foundational to the historic identity of this congregation, your message is, 'Please change now.'

"Help me understand this puzzle."

There was a long, long silence. We rode two whole blocks. We sat at a long traffic light.

Finally, Bob said, "I see what you mean."

"Bob," I said, "I have another puzzle. You teach me—your congregation teaches me—that your best preaching happens on Sunday night. You study the text. You consult the commentaries. You pray for your message. With a simple outline, you share a warm, insightful sermon. Your people leave with what I call handles of help and hope.

"On Sunday morning, you virtually read a long, tedious manuscript sermon. Both you and your people teach me that your preaching on Sunday evening is most helpful. For you, from now on, Sunday morning is Sunday evening. Each Sunday morning, share the best Sunday evening sermon you can. And if, on Sunday evening, you read a manuscript sermon, it won't do that much damage and harm."

That day, I suggested to Bob that he make these two changes in himself, simply and quietly. I suggested to him that people would sense his own flexibility and growth. I encouraged him not to set up a bargain—namely, his saying he would make these two changes if women would be allowed to vote. Bargaining would not help. What would help, what would give his people confidence and assurance that they could change, was that they would sense his own willingness to change, to be flexible.

Some time passed. As I remember, ten to twelve weeks came and went after I shared with the congregation. Gene called me long distance, just before we were to leave for Australia. He said, "Dr. Callahan, would it really work for women to vote in our congregation?"

I said, "Yes, Gene, it will work, and you will be remembered years hence as the person who built the original sanctuary, which is now the chapel, the education building, and the new sanctuary. Most especially, fifty years from now, you will be remembered as the person who built the bridge to the mainland."

Then, I said, "Gene, you will want to deal with the ghost of your mother in some other way." Ghost of mother. You always ask yourself, when someone expends as much energy as Gene has over five years, gathering people out of the woodwork, what more is going on here than is apparent?

The reason we talked long and late that first afternoon is because we were talking about his growing-up years. He was the oldest of four. He was seven years old when his father deserted the family. His mother took her anger, bitterness, and resentment out on her oldest son.

From the time he was seven until he became fifteen, she beat him up, emotionally, physically, spiritually. When he got to be fifteen he was now big enough to beat her up, but rather than do that, he ran away from home, got a job as a carpenter's helper, and worked himself up over the years to his own major building firm.

I said, "Gene, you will want to deal with the ghost of your mother in some other way. It is not fair to her. It is not fair to you. It is not fair to the congregation you dearly love."

Three things happen in that congregation today. One, the bulletin is done on Thursday. Two, every Sunday morning, Bob preaches the best Sunday evening sermon in the area. Three, women vote.

It was in helping that congregation that I discovered the principle I call two for one: *make two changes in yourself for each one change you hope for in other persons.*

Another way I think of the principle is this: be flexible in yourself in two ways for each one way you hope other people will be flexible. Ask of yourself what you ask of others. For each change you hope for in people in your family, at work, or where ever, make two changes in yourself. Do not do this in a bargaining way. Do not say, in effect, that you will make these two changes, if they will make this one. That does not help.

Simply and quietly, make the two changes that help you grow you. As they see your creativity and growth, people gain confidence and assurance that they too can change. Grow yourself forward in two ways for each one way you hope others will grow forward. People take heart from your example.

The spirit of flexibility includes flexibility in oneself, not simply counting on flexibility in others. As pastor, Bob had counted on flexibility in others, and with our conversation that day, he discovered flexibility in himself. We learn a spirit of flexibility, a willingness to explore and experiment. Sometimes, regrettably, we are tempted to learn a spirit of rigidity and sameness.

Flexibility is the ancestor of invention. We learn to puzzle. We learn a spirit of curiosity and interest. We learn a spirit of openness and willingness to try new things. Curiosity gives birth to creativity. With a spirit of flexibility, new ideas emerge.

If we become inflexible with ourselves, we tend to become inflexible with others. Sometimes, our spirit of inflexibility contributes to other people becoming inflexible. We both share and receive rigidity and inflexibility. We develop an unhealthy working relationship. Life becomes complex. Our creativity is diminished.

We cherish flexibility in others. The key for our own growth is our own personal range of flexibility. You can teach yourself flexibility. Think of simple ways your can expand your spirit of flexibility. Consider the simple habits you have. Vary them from time to time. In something as simple as reading the newspaper, some people learn to read it from back to front, and some read it from front to back. Try it a new way. In tying your shoes, we learn to tie one shoe first, then the other. Try it in a new way. In eating a meal, some learn to eat certain foods on the plate in a certain order, almost one at a time. Try a new way. We learn routine travel patterns around our communities. Explore a new way. We sign notes and letters in a certain way. We have been doing it that way for years. Try a new way.

Creativity is discovering some new way. It can be a new way to dig a ditch, a new way to quilt, a new way of washing the clothes, or a new way of painting a house. Creativity is lived out in new discoveries in daily living. Think of simple ways you can expand your spirit of flexibility. As you do so, you are in a stronger position to expand your flexibility in the more complex areas of your life.

The Capacity to Learn in a Rich Variety of Ways

We learn, and have the potential of learning, in seven ways:

- Physical, athletic
- Cognitive, intellectual
- Work project
- Social, relational
- Fad of the moment
- Over against, outcast
- Independent, individualistic

We learn in a rich variety of ways. These seven represent both the richness and diversity of ways in which we discover and learn; they also represent the interpersonal groupings in which we participate. We learn in more ways than simply cognitively and intellectually. We learn in all seven ways.

At many high schools, you will find these groupings. From one high school to the next, from one decade to the next, the groups may vary, the names may change. You can look in a high school yearbook and find the groupings.

Like most groups that have some sense of continuity and stability, each grouping develops its own

- Goals and values
- Customs, habits, and traditions
- Language and communication network
- Leadership and decision-making process
- Sacred places of meeting
- Common, shared vision of the future

There is overlap. The smaller the high school, the more overlap in the groupings. The larger the high school the less overlap, and the more distinct each group is. There is interchange. A given student may be part of one grouping for a time, and then decide to move to another group. The smaller the high school, the easier the interchange. The larger the high school the tougher the transition.

There is multiple participation. A given high school student may participate in more than one grouping at the same time. The smaller the high school, the easier it is to simultaneously participate in more than one group. The larger the high school, the more difficult it is to do so. Although one student may participate in more than one group, these are the primary groupings in most high schools.

These groupings exist in adult life as well, and the possibilities of overlap, interchange, and multiple participation exist with adults too. For example, when I help with a congregation I visit the adult classes. When I walk into the class that calls itself the Workers' Class, I know I have walked into the work project group. When I walk into the class that calls itself the Fellowship Class, I know I have walked into the social, relational grouping. When I walk into the class that calls itself the Kerygma Class, I know I have walked into the intellectual group. That is the only group who can remember how to spell the word.

I walked into one class and they said to me good-naturedly and cheerfully, "Dr. Callahan, we are the group that is against everything in this church." I knew I had walked into the outcast group.

There are distinctive groupings to which we are drawn across our life's pilgrimage. Think of all groups in your community. The athletic and recreational groupings. The intellectual and cognitive groups. The work project, interest, civic, and community groups. The social and fellowship groupings.

The groupings that stir as a fad of the moment, then are gone. The over-against, outcast groups. Think of all the individual, individualistic patterns we create for ourselves. There may be many more groupings in a community, while at the same time these seven are usually present.

We learn in a rich variety of ways. These seven are groupings with which we participate. Equally important, they are the rich variety of ways we discover and learn. We do not learn only in one way. We learn in all seven ways.

We learn in a physical, athletic way. People who play on an athletic team learn much about life. When it is a healthy team, they discover learnings of compassion, hope, community, encouragement, creativity, and health, to mention a few of the learnings that take place as they share together on the team. A wide range of adult groupings, informal and formal, gather around some physical activity—whether it be canoeing, bowling, skiing, hiking, tennis, square dancing, or whatever—and in the process people discover roots, place, and belonging, and learn much about themselves in this life's pilgrimage.

We learn in a cognitive, intellectual way. Using our mind, we study some material, seeking to internalize it into our being. We read, discuss, think in informational ways and, in so doing, we discover facts and figures, the whys and wherefores, and we discover understanding and insight.

We learn in a work-project way. Habitat for Humanity, where we gather to build a house, is a work-project way of learning. In the process of building a house, we learn mission and service, compassion and hope, community and creativity, to mention a few of the learnings that take place. A group of people take on a work project to raise funds for a worthy cause. In doing so, they discover a life of generosity. People assemble in all sorts of ways to do some project together. Art, music, woodworking, sculpturing, quilting are all work-project (in the deepest sense of the word) ways of learning and expressing. Sometimes, people share in these as a group, and frequently people work on their projects individually. Importantly, they discover and grow their creativity.

We learn in a social, relational way. In our interactions in a group, we learn much about the lessons of life. Through the friendships and relationships we develop, we learn much about people and about ourselves.

We learn in short-term, highly intensive, fad-of-the-moment ways. Some fad comes along. We become engrossed in it. We take on the goals and values, the behavior patterns and language of the fad, and in the process we learn about community, leadership, and creativity, to mention some of the learnings that take place. Then, some new fad emerges. We are captivated by it, learn from it, and move on.

We learn in an over-against, outcast way. We stand over against some authority, and we learn much about ourselves and the principles on which we want to base our life. We want some sense of identity and autonomy, and we learn these as we stand over against something.

We learn in independent, individualistic ways that are distinctive for whom each of us is and the particular, specific patterns of learning that we have developed for ourselves.

We learn in all seven ways. For the moment, we may have developed one or two of the seven as the predominant ways in which we have learned to learn. You are not locked into the one or two you have currently developed. You can grow any of the seven forward.

People who have grown the cognitive, intellectual way of learning frequently advance the physical way of learning as they participate in a Habitat for Humanity project. People who have grown the work-project way of learning frequently seek out a relational group, discover roots, place, and belonging, and grow their social way of learning forward.

You are welcome to decide which of these ways of learning you would have fun advancing. Put in place a simple plan that helps you grow forward that way. The more of these ways of learning you grow in yourself, the higher the level of creativity you have. The fuller the range of your learning resources, the stronger the capacity to see the whole, not the parts. The richer the ways of learning, the deeper the creativity.

We can develop our capacity to learn from our mistakes. We can advance our capacity to learn from our achievements. We can benefit from the two-for-one principle. It helps us with a spirit of flexibility. We can grow our capacity to learn in a rich variety of ways.

In Isaiah 65:17 we discover these words: "For behold, I create new heavens and a new earth. . . ." Our God is the Creator God, the God of all creation and all creativity. God relates to us as the God who is creating. The ultimate source of whatever creativity we have is in the creativity of God.

The time in which we live invites our best creativity and imagination, our best searching and questing, our best learning and growing. This is a wilderness time, a pioneering time, a time for sailing. This is not a safe, secure time. This is not a castle time. This is not a docking time, a harbor time. This is not a temple time. This is not a cathedral time. There is no fortress within which we can withdraw.

This is a time for setting sail. Ships are made for sailing, not staying at a dock. A ship is clumsy and awkward at a dock. It rolls and bangs and thuds against the dock. You can steer a ship only when it is underway. When it sits dead in the water, you cannot steer it. Even a powerboat cannot be steered when the engine is dead. The sailor's term is that "the ship is in irons."

'Tis on the ocean that a ship is made to be. There a ship is a thing of beauty as it flies before the wind. May your creativity grow and develop in the same way as you sail through this life. May the winds of creativity stir your soul and give life to your ship.

———————o———————

Merciful and Loving God,
 Help us confess our mistakes and learn from them.
We give You the praise for whatever achievements You have given us.
 Show us how to learn from these achievements.
  Help us make two changes in ourselves for each one change
   we invite in people around us.
 Give us the gift of flexibility.
Lord God, You give us the capacity to learn in a rich variety of ways.
 Help us learn how to learn in these ways.
  Thank You for the gift of creativity.
   In the name of Christ, we pray. Amen.

13

HEALTH

I WAS HELPING one congregation. We were in the sanctuary praying for the future of that church. They have a remarkable stained glass window of Christ, standing at the door knocking. Once you have seen it, you remember the picture, the window, the biblical image.

In an earlier time, the understanding of the window was that Christ stood at the door knocking, hoping someone would hear the knock, and come to the door, open the door, and invite Christ *in*. Some people made much of the fact that there was no latchkey, no door knob on the outside of the door, and we therefore would be the ones to hear the knock, and come to the door, open the door, and invite Christ *in* to our lives.

It dawned on me that day, sunlight streaming through the window, what the picture, the window, the biblical image means in our time.

We live in one of the richest ages for mission the Christian movement has ever known. What the picture, the window, the biblical image means is that Christ stands at the door knocking, hoping we will hear the knock, come to the door, and open the door, so that Christ can invite us *out*.

It is no longer that we invite Christ in. Christ invites us out. Where does Christ live and die and rise again and again? Among the human hurts and hopes of the people all around us. God is in the world. Whenever we are in the world, God is in us. Whenever we are not in the world, God is in the world.

The text says, "For God so loved the world." It does not say, "For God so loved the church." It is not that we find Christ, and then go and do the mission. It is in the mission that we discover Christ.

Valuing the Gift of Life

God invites us to a life of health and wellness, not illness and sickness. Amidst the toothaches and tonsils, the colds and the illnesses, the pain and weight of life that abound, we can grow forward the resources for a life of health and wellness by

○ Appreciating and valuing the gift of life

○ Having some capacity to deal with the presence of death

○ Developing a positive attitude about our health

○ Feeding our spirit in mission and prayer

Life is our friend. The gift of life is extraordinary. The joy of living, the rising of the sun, the wonder of being alive, the closeness of loved ones, the miracle that you and I are alive, the possibilities before us, all of this is amazing. Life is among the best gifts we will ever be given. We could not have been born. We could have never existed. Life is not to be taken for granted. We are here! We live! We move and breathe and have our being. Life is our friend.

Part of living a strong, healthy life is the capacity to value and cherish life. Sometimes, we spend and waste our lives as though we had a million years. We move through life hardly noticing who or what is around us. The years slip like sand through our fingers. We place ourselves on a merry-go-round of busyness that whirls faster and faster as the years pass. We throw some of our best years to the wind.

We become preoccupied with our education. We get caught up in our vocation. We advance from one position to another, moving higher in our company. We buy this and build that. Project after project is achieved. They blur in our minds as we look back on them; they happen so quickly. We are busy in our community. We participate in worthwhile causes. We help with this civic cause and that community activity. The days and weeks swiftly pass. The years come and go. We are so busy.

Then, some precipitating event happens. We are reminded of how precious and precarious life is. We rediscover the priceless, cherished value of our life, and we are, once again, attuned to the gift of life with which God blesses us. We claim the gift of life.

Yes, we sometimes wonder about the connection of life and death. It does seem strange that we are born to die. Why are we not born to live forever? The old argument that we die to make space on the planet for new people is somehow hollow when one considers one's own death. It simply doesn't work to say we die to save space. It could have been God's plan that people who are born live on rather than die. The fact that we are given life, and that at the end there is death is, for some, an irony, a cruel joke.

It helps to focus on the fact that we might not have been born. It helps to know the other choice could have been that we were never born, that we were never alive, even to worry about death. We can be grateful we have been given this glimpse of life, fleeting and fragile as it may be, as a gift, to cherish its richness and vitality, to cling desperately to its wondrous beauty and depth. We can appreciate and value the gift of life.

Dealing with the Presence of Death

Life is our friend. Death is our neighbor. Death is near—not, I think, as a friend, however sentimental and romantic some would try to make death appear. Death waits for its time. It comes in many ways, sometimes softly, silently. Other times, death comes with a loud crash. Quick and gone. Sometimes death comes in terrible agony, in suffering and pain, lingering long. Death comes in many forms, and it comes to us all.

Part of living a strong, healthy life is the capacity to deal, as best we can, with death. We develop our capacity for dealing with death as it comes to us in the small and great tragedies that happen, whether in our community or around the planet. We are casually reading the evening paper. On page three there is a story about an elementary school teacher who, having taught for thirty years, a legend among children and parents for three generations, died the day before in a nearby hospital. We knew her only in passing. We think to ourselves how different the community will be now without her, and we wonder how her family, her former students, and their parents are doing. We know death.

There is a car accident, out on the highway at a treacherous intersection. We have had close calls at that intersection ourselves. This time, according to the reports, two cars crashed nearly head on. We do not know the families. All were killed. No—one person barely clings to life in the intensive care unit of a local hospital. Our compassion and sympathy are stirred. We know death.

There is a catastrophe somewhere on the planet. A dam broke, caused by the downpour of drenching rains in the nearby mountains. Hundreds are dead. The news reports the horror and tragedy. The pictures are grim and grisly. We know death. Our generosity is touched. We send aid to help those who survive. In another news report we learn of persons slowly dying of hunger and disease on the other side of the globe. We know death walks among all peoples. We share our help, and, in doing so, we come to terms with death.

We deal with death, sometimes well and sometimes not so well, as we experience the death of our close friends and our loved ones. We see them slowly waste away and die in the hospital. Or we search frantically for a child at a lake, hoping against hope she has not drowned. Or we wish there had been a railroad signal at a crossing, and now we run up and down the tracks, seeing the littered and mangled bodies, searching for one's family among the debris and carnage. Or we watch the last gasp of a loved one in his bed at home. We stand at his grave. All these experiences of death trouble us.

We lose family. We miss friends. As the years pass, more and more of the people we love dearest and best cross over the river to the other side. We are left more and more alone. We discover we know more and more people who have died. These experiences remind us of the future of our own death.

We deal with our own death. It is sometimes difficult to type that sentence, let alone read it. We do die. Death is not simply a concept. It is a reality with which we wrestle. It is no longer the death of strangers somewhere across the planet, or of friends and even loved ones close to us. It is very close to home. We, you and I, die.

We deal with death in various ways. We try to ignore its reality. That is easier when we are young. We try to run from it, living a life of escapism in this fad or that foolishness, trying to make every minute of pleasure count. We try to defeat it, take it head on, wrestle it to the ground by our striving and achieving.

We try to outlive its knock on our door. We look to life beyond the river. Sometimes, we try to claim that death is but an illusion. Some suggest that this life is the illusion, and the real life is yet to come. We frequently choose to stay busy, with a hectic, restless pace of activities, so as to lose any sense of death in the bustle of the moment.

Midlife crisis has something to do with death. People sense they have lived half their lives, that they are on the other side, and at times they feel they are moving faster toward the end. On occasion, all sorts of simple, sometimes bizarre, forms of behavior occur at that point. People make those last, feeble efforts to recover their youth, to pretend that life is not now half over.

In an ancient manuscript it is written, Death is God. There was, years ago, a movement some referred to as the God is Dead movement. That movement lasted a short time. The ancient manuscript would have us believe that the more profound, troubling truth is that death is God, that the final god of this life is death, that the ultimate reality is death, that the only constant is the fact of death. It is an interesting point of view.

Death comes to us. My wisdom teaches me that our capacity to deal with death, to accept it as part of living, has something to do with living a whole, healthy life. That does not mean we figure out a solution. It simply means that, as best we can, we are from time to time at peace with the fact that we are given the rich, full gift, the good friend of life, and that with it comes its neighbor, death. Let us not be quietly frantic, nor subtly ignore, nor run from, nor worry too much about death.

There are three choices with death. The first choice: in the end, death wins. We are born to die. When we are born, we start to die. Some of us spend half our lives worrying about our death. Were we not born, there would be nothing to worry about.

The second choice: in the end, we win. When we are born, we start to strive. Some of us spend half our lives striving to win over death. Our bargain with God is that we do good works, are deeply committed, faithful, and loyal, and we earn from God the ability to not die. By being good, by doing helpful things, by being dedicated Christians, we seek to create the illusion we will not die.

If by chance we do die, we hope, by our good works, that we earn our immortality and we do not really die. The irony is, we try to earn what God has already given us—is seeking to give us each day. We are saved by faith, not by our own righteousness, not by our own doing. It is the gift of God. We are alive, and this is not our own doing; it is the gift of God.

The third choice: in the end, God wins. We are born to live, to serve. When we are born, we start to live, we start to serve. We are given the gift of life. It is not our own doing. With the gift of life given from God, we grow forward whole, healthy lives.

With each kind deed, each serving act, each selfless mission, we participate in the mission of God. Compassion, kindness, mercy, and hope do not perish. These live on. Live the gift of life, for now. This day. The mission of God is eternal. Do not worry about death. Living life is better than worrying about death. It is hard to do both at the same time.

The capacity to appreciate life has something to do with the capacity to deal with death. Those who appreciate life are better able to deal with death. Those who do not value the gift of life have greater trouble dealing with death. Were it not for the gift of life, we would not be alive to worry about our death. Give thanks to God for life. Be at peace about death.

Developing a Positive Attitude

God invites us to have a positive attitude about our health. Some people have a negative attitude about their health. They behave self-destructively. Mostly, they have a negative attitude about their life and themselves. If we have a positive attitude about our life and ourselves, we tend to do better with our health. God gives us the gift of life, God gives us the victory over death, and God gives us this body with which to live this life.

We are whole beings, whole persons. We are intellectual beings, who think and reflect, ponder and consider, discover and create; we search for meaning and purpose in our lives. We are emotional beings, who love and laugh, feel joy and sorrow, experience fear and anger, guilt and forgiveness; we share compassion and community. We are willful beings, who have a sense of will and direction, purpose and focus, determination and resolution; we seek to move forward in our lives. We are spiritual beings, with yearnings and longings, strivings and aspirations, vision and hope, who search for that which is holy and sacred in this life and the next.

We are physical beings, who breathe and move, walk and run, lift and carry, hunger and thirst, sleep and wake. We enjoy good health and well-being, and then illness and sickness may come to us. We care for, look after, and nourish our physical body. We are more than our body, and we are our body. We cannot live this life apart from our body. We are whole beings in our mind, our emotions, our will, our soul, and our body. God invites us to develop healthy minds, emotions, will, soul, and body—to have a positive attitude about our whole being.

We accept graciously, gratefully, thankfully the gift of life. We treasure this priceless gift. We are good stewards of it. We see the precious gift for what it is. It is not that we hoard it. We receive the gift with awe and appreciation, wonder and joy. We grow and advance the gift of life with which God has blessed us. Likewise, we receive the gift of our body with awe and appreciation. We grow and advance the gift of our body.

It is helpful for us to eat and exercise so as to contribute to our health, not for vain, egotistical reasons so that we somehow "look good," whatever that may mean. We are invited to care for our body as a gift of God, in the same way one would care for a precious gift. This body is the one body we are given as a gift for this lifetime. There is no other in this life.

This body is a sacrament, an outward and visible sign of the inner and invisible grace, creativity, and creation of God. This body is a sign of grace, compassion, community, and hope. This body is the tangible sign of God's love and grace with us. God gives us this body that we might live in this life.

Self-destruction is the result of low self-esteem. Sometimes we engage in eating patterns that are self-destructive. Other times, we eat to assure ourselves we will survive, but in the process we destroy ourselves. We overeat and create all sorts of problems for our health.

It is an interesting journey on which we travel. Our spaceship, if you will, is the body God has given us. We are invited to care for this gift as best we can, in our eating and in our exercise. Sometimes, we overeat and sometimes we undereat. Eating with a sense of balance is an art we can discover and learn. Sometimes, we overexercise and sometimes we under-exercise. Caring for our physical health is an art we can learn and develop. We are better able to this if we have a positive attitude about our health.

Feeding My Spirit in Mission and Prayer

We feed our whole being as we live a life of mission and prayer. These two, mission and prayer, are good friends. Where one is, the other is also. Mission is a form of prayer. Prayer is a form of mission. It is hard to have one without the other. God invites us to feed our spirit, our whole being creatively and healthfully. There is a correlation between the health of our mind, our emotions, our will, our soul, and our body. You and I are whole persons. We feed our spirit in mission and prayer, and in so doing we care for our health and our whole being.

We feed our spirit as we serve in mission. In our giving, we are nourished. In our sharing in mission, we discover we nourish our own being. Sometimes, if we become too preoccupied with ourselves, if we focus too much on our own concerns, if we worry too much about our own health, it is then that we are likely to get sick. Sometimes, if we worry too much about something, it happens. As we give ourselves in mission, we feed ourselves in our spirit and nurture the health of our whole being.

It is not that we first feed our spirit in prayer and then go out and share ourselves in mission. It is in accepting Christ's invitation *out* in mission that we feed our spirit. It is not that we first draw close to God in prayer and then go out and share in mission. Sometimes, that is the way it happens. More often, it is as we share in the mission that we draw close to God. God is in the mission. When we are in the mission, we are close to God.

Sharing in mission is a way of praying. The mission is a prayer lifted to God. As we share in mission, we pray without ceasing. Our prayer life is built on more than resolutions to be sure to pray steadfastly, regularly, daily, weekly, monthly, year in and year out. Yes, we do have our times of prayer and devotion, in the quiet, away from the chaos and confusion around us. These times away feed our spirit. We experience a sense of serenity and peace. We draw close to the grace of God. We feel ourselves in the presence of the Holy. These times of prayer are central to our health and well-being. We deepen our spirituality and discover the richness and fullness of the grace of God.

Our prayer life is built on mission. We pray as we share in mission. Mission is prayer in action. As we share in mission, we nourish our whole being. We nurture a healthy body, helpful emotions, a constructive mind, and a rich, full spirit. Mission stirs prayer. Prayer stirs mission. We discover our full health in mission and prayer.

Our life of mission and prayer is active in ways that match with who we are. Some of us share and pray in the short term, intensely, near the time at hand. Some of us share and pray regularly and routinely, day by day. We each discover a life of prayer, times of praying, and ways of praying that help us sense the presence of God. Our prayers nourish who we are and whose we are. We feed our being, our spirit one day at a time. We discover the richness and fullness of this day—prayerfully and in healing.

God gives us the gift of life. We are invited to appreciate and value the gift of life. God gives us victory over death. We are invited to have a positive attitude about our health. God encourages us to feed our spirit in mission and prayer.

We live the gift of life, the gift of this day, as a sacrament. We care for, nurture, and nourish, our whole being—mind, emotions, will, soul, and body—this day, healthfully and wholesomely. This one day, we live a life of prayer. This one day, we live a sacramental life. This one day, we live in healthy, wholesome ways.

———————— o ————————

God of life, for the gift of this life we are grateful.

We are amazed to be alive.

For Your victory over death, we are most thankful.

We pray You will bring us into Your Kingdom in the life to come.

Help us develop a positive attitude about our health.

Grant that we might care well for the life You give us.

Help us, with mission and prayer, to feed our spirit. Amen.

14

GENEROSITY

"TOM IS GENEROUS." "It is amazing all of the people Tom helps." "Tom is among the most generous people I know." "Tom assists more people than anyone I have ever known." When people think of Tom, they think of his generosity. Tom is a legend for his amazing generosity.

Tom grew up poor. His father kicked him and his brother out of the home when they were still in elementary school. They were young and on their own. They had a tough time. They fared for themselves for a while, doing this or that odd job. Finally, they found steady work on a farm. Mostly, they put themselves through grade school. It was anything but easy.

High school ensued. College followed. Graduate school followed beyond that. There were, to be sure, scholarships and loans. It was mostly working multiple jobs, part-time and full-time, long hours, hard work. Studying late at night and on into the early morning. There was not a lot of time for much else.

There was laughter. There were good times. There were close friendships and new family. There were discoveries and insights. There was no resentment, no bitterness. There was no lamenting, complaining, whining, bemoaning. There was no bad-mouthing: woe is me, poor little me. There was graciousness and kindness.

It was more than making the best of a bad deal in life. It was moving on. Building one's life, as best one could, given the resources at hand. Tom's gift for understanding, loving, accepting, being generous with those who were down and out came from his having been there. He knew what it was like.

He never seemed to have much money. What he had, he gave away. It was not, I think, that he was a soft touch. It was more as if he had a deep compassion and a strong spirit of generosity. He would help in whatever ways he could. He gave his time. He provided food. He helped with some money. He provided a bed for the night and a bus ticket home. He loved people. The lives he touched, the people he helped, the families who were restored, the youths who were inspired, their number is legion.

Modest Financial Needs

One key, one possibility, for a whole, healthy life is generosity. God invites us to a life of generosity, not grabbing and hoarding, conserving and holding, protecting and preserving. Sharing the grace of generosity is one of the rare gifts in life. We are at our best when, amidst the scarcity and plenty, the shortness and the fullness, all of which abound, we discover the sources for a life of generosity and giving by

- ○ Living a life of modest needs
- ○ Valuing ourselves in more ways than money
- ○ Developing our financial resources
- ○ Sharing our blessings with many persons and causes

We all have some financial, housing, transportation, clothing, food, and fun needs. Sometimes, we become preoccupied with our financial needs. Finances become too much of the focus of our lives. Life gets out of balance. The need for finances becomes excessive. We begin, excessively, to conserve and hold, protect and preserve our meager financial resources. Grabbing and hoarding enter our lives. We are no longer generous.

Some people, like Tom, grow up in abject poverty and, for whatever reasons, become persons of considerable generosity. Other people grow up in comparable poverty and, for whatever reasons, develop a driving obsession to grab and hoard all they can get. For them, the fear and pain of those early years creates a compulsive determination to never be poor again, to acquire all they can get. They never seem to have enough.

How much is enough? Ask yourself, "How much money is really enough?" For some people, financial needs are modest. For them, life is more than possessions, wealth, and money. For other people, financial needs are never satisfied. For them, being satisfied is always one more dollar over the horizon. They become almost compulsive about money.

In a barter economy, possessions and wealth are measured in harvests and crops, cows and cheese, land and water. In a barter economy, one's wealth and purchasing power exists at the time of the harvest. There is not much income during the rest of the year. Most of the income happens once a year.

In a cash economy, one's wealth is measured in cash. I put my way through school digging ditches, running a ninety-pound jackhammer, building roads and highways. I worked up to being a form setter. We received our pay each Friday in a little brown envelope, in cash. In a cash economy, one's purchasing power tends to happen weekly. The rent, the insurance, the car, the groceries are paid weekly.

In a check-and-credit-card economy, income is received in checks that come to people semimonthly or monthly. People usually expend much of their purchasing power monthly in response to credit card statements that show up monthly. In an automatic-transfer economy, income is received and expended in computer transactions that happen in nanoseconds.

There are people with whom I have had the privilege of sharing who are now in their eighties, who grew up in a barter economy, learned how to live in a cash economy, found their way through a check-and-credit-card economy, and now live in an automatic-transfer economy. They have made an amazing pilgrimage.

Financial resources are helpful in whatever form they come. What is really at stake is the income and purchasing power that people have. How much is enough? This is an intriguing question. In a barter economy, the question is how many crops and cows, how much cheese is enough. In a cash economy, it is how much money. In a check-and-credit-card economy, it is how much of a paycheck is enough. In an automatic-transfer economy, it is how much in one's computer accounts is enough.

In whatever form, ask yourself: How much in the way of income and possessions, purchasing power and wealth do you need? Consider living a life of modest financial needs. Given that objective, think through the income and assets that help you achieve your objective. What constitutes a life of modest financial needs varies from one person to the next. The actual amount of purchasing power and wealth to achieve the objective also varies from one point in life to the next.

The art is to decide on a reasonable objective and move toward it. The way forward is not to put yourself in the position of simply thinking that you need more money. "More" is a setup to fail. More creates a never-ending horizon of failure. We can never achieve more. More is always one "more" over the horizon. What we can do is assess our needs and develop a reasonable objective toward which we can head.

When we consider an objective of modest financial needs, it is helpful to distinguish between our needs and our wants. We can focus on our needs. We can give less attention to our wants. Sometimes, I think our wants are the devil's way of distracting us from what is really important in life. Regrettably, we are sometimes drawn to the question, "How much money will make me happy?" It is the wrong question. No amount of money will make us happy. We can acquire all the money we could imagine wanting, and if we did we would still not be happy. Money does not buy happiness.

When we live a life of modest financial needs, when we focus on our needs, we avoid being consumed by our wants. Sometimes we allow ourselves to become preoccupied by our wants. We strive and struggle. We work long hours and longer years. We take time away from family and friends. We expend massive physical, emotional, mental, and spiritual energies to earn enough to satisfy our wants. Only to discover this: our wants expand faster than we can satisfy them. It is a never-ending merry-go-round, one that goes faster and faster, as the years pass in a blur and haze.

We live a life of modest financial needs so that we can have some time and energy for living life. In I Timothy 6:10 (NASB) we discover these words: "For the love of money is a root of all sorts of evil, and some by longing for it have wandered away from the faith. . . ."

The key words are *love* and *longing*. The problem is not in the money itself, but in our love of and longing for money. The longing has caused some to wander from the faith. The objection is not to money. The problem is getting so caught up in money that we wander from the faith, that we wander from life, that we miss out on life. Have this confidence: God provides for your needs.

Valuing Yourself

We have all learned attitudes, values, and behavior patterns about money. Our culture is obsessed with money. The culture teaches us the message that money is prestige. With money, we imagine we are looked up to, are well thought of, have the perks, the prerogatives, the pedestal of importance. With money, we are somebody.

The culture teaches us that money is power. With money, we picture that we have power and authority, leverage and influence. With money we are able to command and control, dictate and dominate.

The culture teaches us that money is security. With money, we imagine we are secure against the uncertainties of the times. We are able to hedge our bets against calamities in the culture.

What the culture teaches us is true—for the culture. In our current culture, if people have money, the culture does confer on them cultural prestige, cultural power, and cultural security. In the current culture, we are somebody. The culture values people with money.

But, simply because the culture values us, does that mean we value ourselves? All that happens when we have money is that the culture values
us. We may or may not value ourselves, even amidst the cultural prestige,
power, and security bestowed on us.

Is the source of valuing ourselves to be found in the culture's goals and
values, customs, habits, and traditions? It is an interesting question. Valuing oneself is internal, not external. Ultimately, we value ourselves inside
us. Value is not finally dependent on what other people think of us,
though we do spend a lot of time focusing on that. Value is finally what
we conclude about ourselves.

Confirm your value. Trust your value. Have confidence that your value
is deeper and fuller than the culture can ever confer. Believe in yourself,
at the deepest level of human existence. Say to yourself

> I value myself as a child of God.
> I value myself in my growing and developing.
> I value myself in the mission I am sharing.
> I value myself because my life is counting well.
> God values me for who I am.

We have value in the sight of God, not for what we acquire and achieve,
attain and accomplish but for who we are and whose we are.

God invites us to receive God's love. God invites us to accept ourselves.
This is not always easy to do, because we know ourselves pretty well. God
invites us to value what is important in life. Know this. Have confidence
in this.

> The love of God is renewing.
> The power of God is astonishing.
> The grace of God is amazing.
> The purpose of God is moving.
> The hope of God overcomes all.
> God values you and your life.
> Thanks be to God.

Developing Financial Resources

God invites us to develop our financial resources. God encourages us not
to be too preoccupied with them. At the same time, God encourages us
not to neglect them. In Matthew 6:21 we discover these words: "Where
your treasure is, there will your heart be also." I think it is also true that
where your heart is, there will your treasure be also.

Where our deepest yearnings and longings, our compassion and our passion focus, there we invest our treasure. Wherever we place our treasure is where our heart is also. We invest our lives, and our financial resources in ways that reinforce one another.

Some people grow up poor and never want to be poor again. The fear of being poor drives some people to develop their financial resources, and they do develop considerable wealth. The fear of being poor is still with them. For all their money and riches, the ghost of poorness is present.

The problem is not in the poorness. It is in the fear. The fear of being poor has more to do with fear than it has with being poor. The way forward is to focus on healthy ways of dealing with fear, not ways of dealing with being poor.

We develop our financial resources not with any thought that fear will be dispelled. Rather, we develop our financial resources to help people. We invest our resources in ways that help others. In so doing, we become less preoccupied with ourselves, and therefore less preoccupied with our fear.

We are invited to develop and grow, advance and build our financial resources. We are not asked to grab and hoard, conserve and hold, protect and preserve our financial resources. Regrettably, people who have a conserving, holding approach to their finances develop a conserving, holding approach to life. Someone says, "I am doing the best I can to hoard and hold, protect and preserve my meager financial resources." They are headed to hoarding and holding, protecting and preserving their meager life resources.

What we do with our money is what we do with our life. What we do with our life is what we do with our money. The person who is developing, growing, advancing, building his or her financial resources is also going about the business of growing and developing his or her life.

Growing yields growing. Meager yields meager. People who hoard and hold their meager financial resources live that way, and they give that way. When they give, they do so reluctantly. There is a meagerness of spirit in their giving. Some people who have meager financial resources do not hoard and hold what they have; they give with a spirit of generosity. God invites us to give out of our generosity, not our income. People who grow their finances grow their lives and grow their generosity.

Develop your financial resources thoughtfully and reasonably with some sense of your future, some sense of advancing your well-being. Do so with wisdom and compassion. We are not invited to a life of "sparsimosity." We are invited to a life of generosity.

Mission is more important than money. The mission is not the money. The mission is more enduring than that. If our hearts are in mission, then money takes its rightful place. We can develop our financial resources not for our own sake but for the sake of the mission. If the necessities of the mission are clear, the necessities of life are clear.

Our enduring hope is in mission, not in money. Some people have a vacuum of hope in their lives, so they focus on money and materialism. They do not wrestle, finally, with materialism. They wrestle with a lack of hope. When hope is dim, vague, gone, people look for hope somewhere. They look for specific and concrete sources of hope. Lacking them, they sometimes look for hope in the fragile, momentary thing called money.

Have this confidence: people give money to people. We are invited to develop our financial resources in such a way that we can be of help with people. In doing so, we encourage others to be of help with people.

Sharing Blessings

Living is giving. We live as we breathe. We live as we give. Without breathing, there is no life. Without giving, there is no life. Giving is as natural as breathing. Giving is the breath of the soul.

People have a genuine spirit of generosity. Our nature is generosity because we are created in the image and likeness of God. Our generosity is not because of anything we have done. Our spirit of generosity is a gift from God. God's nature is amazing grace and generosity. When we live forward to our best true selves, we share life with grace and generosity.

We live forward or downward to the expectancies we have of ourselves. If we think of ourselves as stingy and selfish, we won't be disappointed. It is a self-fulfilling prophecy. If we think of ourselves as gracious and generous, we won't be disappointed. We share life and the blessings God gives us with generosity.

The song has it, "I count my blessings one by one." It is well to know that we have what we have, that we are what we are, that we do what we do, as blessings from God. It is helpful, as the song suggests, to count our blessings. We discover how many blessings we have been given. The song could have a verse like, "I share my blessings one by one." It is helpful to count our blessings. It is more helpful to share our blessings.

To be sure, we are grateful for the bountiful meals we enjoy. We also share our blessings by finding a way to pass them on. Bev donates canned food to the Drive Against Hunger. Jim and Earlene help serve meals at a homeless shelter. Lori's children help her take Meals on Wheels to elderly neighbors in the community.

We give thanks for a warm, secure home. We also share our blessings by finding a way to pass them on. Fred and Sandy donate blankets to help flood victims. Tom and Marti help construct Habitat for Humanity homes. Sandy shows friends how to make sleeping bags for the homeless. Countless persons contribute to funds that help people with the costs of heating their homes during the coldest months.

We have the sense we are growing, developing in life. We have some control over where we are headed, not much, but some. Our lives are counting in worthwhile ways. We are part of a winning cause. Then we are generous.

Tom had the sense that he was advancing and building his life effectively. He had the sense of being surrounded by the love of God. He had the confidence that his life counted, was worthwhile and constructive. He had a sense of where he was headed in life. He knew he was part of a winning cause. He shared his generosity in amazing ways.

By contrast, when we have the sense that our lives are standing still, not growing, that we have no control over where we are headed, that our lives are wasting away, that life feels like a sinking ship, then we are less generous. Sometimes, we are self-centered, striving, despairing, vain. Our fear gets the best of us. We feel distant from God's love. The more frightened and fearful we are, the more selfish we become. Stingy and selfish behavior patterns are our ways of trying to protect ourselves from our fear.

Gracious receivers are generous givers. As we graciously receive the grace of God, we have the confidence that we can be generous givers. Reassurance comes from God. When we try to reassure ourselves, we take it upon ourselves to deal with our fear by ourselves. Our fear gets the best of us. We try harder to deal with our fear. We develop a fear of our fear. We try harder yet.

We receive the love of God. God's love pours forth to us, tumbling, rushing, spilling over like rivers in the wilderness. With the extraordinary love of God, we accept our fear. We receive the calming, restoring spirit of God. We receive the healing, renewing grace of God. We receive God's generosity. We become generous givers.

We live lives of modest financial needs. We value ourselves in more ways than money. We develop our financial resources. We share our blessings with many persons and causes.

———○———

Mission is stronger than money.
  We are the people of mission.
Service is stronger than survival.
  We are the people of service.
Sacrifice is stronger than striving.
  We are the people of sacrifice.
Generosity is stronger than getting.
  We are the giving people.
The cross of Calvary is stronger than the empires of the world.
  We are the people of the cross.
The crucified Christ is stronger than the powers of this world.
  We are the people of the crucified Christ.
The generosity of God is stronger than the strivings of humankind.
  We are the people of grace.
    We are the people of compassion.
    We are the people of generosity. Amen.

15

GROWING THE KEYS
IN YOUR LIFE

I WAS WATCHING the Final Four in college basketball. That particular year, exciting, compelling basketball was being played in the final stages of the National College Basketball Tournament. Toward half-time of one game, with a fast break and a full-court press, a team got ahead by twenty-plus points. They were acting on their game plan. They played an extra-ordinary first half. Their teamwork, speed, and ability were amazing to behold.

They came out after half-time, and in the third quarter they began to lose their lead and fall disastrously behind. It was as if they were some other team.

The announcer of the game asked the coach-announcer what had happened. The coach-announcer said, "I've always taught my teams that we play to win. In the first and second quarters of the game, with their fast break and full-court press, this team played to win. In the third quarter, they began to play to avoid losing, and they got off their game, and that is why they fell behind."

I thought about that game for a long time. I know people who *act*, who move forward, who live life with confidence and assurance: "I play to win." Their spirit is: "I count on accomplishing something worthwhile with my life." They live not with a self-centered sense of self-promotion and self-aggrandizement but with a spirit that says, "I want my life to count, in enduring, lasting ways. I count on making some constructive difference for the betterment of my family, my friends, for the advancement of humankind. I am growing my life now."

I know some people whose life, regrettably, seems to say, "I play to avoid losing." There is no growth forward. They take a kind of retrenchment or retreat approach to life, and there is a sense of underlying despair. They may even be "ahead in the game, twenty-plus points." But they have developed a cautious, holding, trying-to-avoid-losing stance. They are off their game.

I know people whose approach to life is, "I play to lose." For various reasons, they have developed an identity of failure. There is no action, no growth forward. Just about the time they get near success, they marshal all their resources and competencies to ensure they fail once again. For them to succeed would create an identity crisis. It would challenge their notion that they always fail. So they ensure that they lose yet again.

I know people whose approach to life is, "I am not certain I plan to leave the locker room. It is safer and more secure here." But there is little life and no action in a locker room. The game is won on the field, not in the locker room. The locker room is not where life is lived out. Some preparation can take place in a locker room, but the game itself is played on the field.

The truth is, all of us sometimes—at various stages of life, even on various days of the week—live life all these ways:

I play to win.

I play to avoid losing.

I play to lose.

I am not certain I plan to leave the locker room.

We find ourselves, from time to time, involved with each.

When we live "I play to win," we help those around us. Innately, we know we are created by God to live life this way. We are drawn to people who live with this integrity and spirit. When we live life any of the other three ways, routinely, dully, we do not help those around us. They already have enough difficulty with those other three ways in their own lives.

Misery may love company, but people are smart enough to know they do not need the mixed blessing of a person who is in no better shape than they are, and who is not advancing his life. When we act on our life, when we grow our life, we help other persons act on and grow their life.

Expand a Strength

In Romans 12:2 we find these words: ". . . be ye transformed by the renewing of your mind. . . ." How we think of ourselves is how we behave. These four steps are a helpful way forward:

1. Claim your strengths.
2. Expand one of your current strengths.
3. Add one new strength.
4. Act on your future.

God encourages us to expand our strengths. Look at the twelve keys. Do the first step. Claim your strengths. We discussed this step in Chapter One.

Now, advance to the second step. Expand one of your current strengths. Take one key you are now carrying out really well. Grow it forward. Expand a strength you really have, not one you wish you had. If you look for the strengths you wish you had, you miss the strengths you really have.

After coaching our church basketball team for four years, I said to my guys, "No more."

Those of you involved in coaching know the investment of time it takes each week: the Tuesday night practice, the Thursday night practice, scouting the other teams, playing the game on Saturday.

My schedule of teaching and research, writing and speaking, and consulting had become so complicated around the country and across the world that some things had to give way. So I said to my guys, "It's been a grand four years, but I can't do it anymore."

My guys said to me, "Coach, we're all going to be seniors in high school this coming year. *Coach us one more year.*" That was a plaintive plea. We had been good family with one another. We were a good team. I wondered, "Could I do it one more year?"

Julie and I talked. It occurred to us that I might find time to do a Thursday night practice and coach the games on Saturday. There would be no Tuesday night practice. There would be no scouting the other teams. On that basis, I said to my guys, "I'll coach one more year."

I was wise enough to know that, if halfway through the season we were not winning our share of games, my guys would be back at me. We would end up with a Tuesday night practice, a makeup Wednesday night practice, the Thursday night practice, scouting the other teams, and playing the games on Saturday. I would be involved even more intensely and extensively than before.

I thought, what do we have going for us that will help us, with one practice and no scouting, to do as well as we have in our previous seasons? It had been sitting in front of me for four years. I had not seen it. My guys were the best *football* team in the county.

Since seventh grade, they had been in spring football practices, illegal summer football practices, the legal summer practices. They had played football all season long. They came to me, each year, at the start of basketball season, as the best football players in the county.

So, in the first Thursday practice, I said to my guys, "This season there are three steps to our offense and our defense. Here is our basket. Sometimes, when we shoot at our basket and miss, someone on the other team is unfortunate enough, unlucky enough to get the rebound.

"Step one: I want the two of you who are nearest him to converge on him as though he were a quarterback seeking to throw a long pass down field. Intimidate him, terrify him, help him know that his life's future—and that of his children and grandchildren—rests on his lateraling sideways. Any attempt downfield puts his future in considerable jeopardy.

"Step two: that gives the other three of you time to set up our secondary zone pass defense, like you learned to run in seventh grade football and have run every year since. The half-court mark of the basketball court is now the fifty-yard line. Set up on our side of the fifty-yard line.

"Step three: intercept the second pass downfield, drive for the basket, make the lay-up, and turn right around and do the same three steps again, as they *try* to throw it in from out of bounds.

"This court is now a football field. We are no longer going to go meekly, mildly clear down to the other end of the field and set up a basketball two-one-two zone defense we haven't figured out to run in four years anyway. We are going to play as much of the game as possible in our end of the field."

My guys liked this approach to the game. It matched with their strengths. They rose to it. They loved it. They thrived on it.

There is one problem with this approach to the game. It is spelled *f-o-u-l-s*. I was much embarrassed during the third game of the season when one of my guys fouled out before half-time. I was even more embarrassed when, as he came to the bench, my bench cleared itself and welcomed him as though he were some kind of conquering hero. I was even more embarrassed because our stands were cheering.

From that game on, whenever a foul was called on one of my team, my bench and our stands cheered. The other coaches would look down the way and shake their heads, wondering what we were doing. Each Thursday practice I said to my guys, "Give up the cross-body blocks. Quit tackling their players. We don't touch them. We don't tackle them. In that sense, this is basketball. We simply terrify and intimidate them. We force them to lateral the ball. We intercept that second pass, drive to the basket, make the lay-up, and turn right around and do it again."

The last game of the season, we got to play the goliaths of the league. They never practiced. They played in three other leagues. They played basketball the whole week long. I'm convinced they never had their tennis shoes off once during the whole season. If you stood downwind from them, you would know what I mean.

So here we were, with five minutes remaining in the fourth quarter, and all my guys except three had fouled out.

It was in that game I learned you could finish a game with however many were left. I had always known the rule that you had to have five to start a game. We sometimes worried whether we would have five to start. It was in that game I learned, in the rules of that particular league, you could finish with however many players were left. I began to wonder, "Now, if we get down to one, how does he pass the ball in to himself from out of bounds?"

We finished the last five minutes of the fourth quarter, playing three against the five goliaths of the league. We beat that team 71 to 63.

Their coach had not prepared them for us. They had never seen basketball played the way we played the game. We had three steps. We consistently did those three steps. We played the game the way we could play best.

When the game was over, we ended up a writhing mass of humanity on the floor, hugging and carrying on. (More injuries occur at that point in a game than any other.) We finally gathered ourselves from the floor and were standing around cheering and carrying on in a circle. My guys said to me, "Coach, we're all going away to college this coming year, but we'll all come home on Saturday, if you'll *coach us one more year.*"

In that one season, my guys played their best. They contributed more speed, quickness, teamwork, energy, and perspiration than all four previous seasons together. They played each game to their fullest, and then some. Their attitude, their action, their accomplishments were amazing to behold. They were building on their strengths, doing what they knew how to do best.

I learned an important lesson in life that season. If we look for the strengths we wish we had, we miss the strengths we really have. I had spent four years looking for basketball strengths. I had missed the strengths we really had: football strengths. As incongruous as it may seem, sometimes God plants us on a basketball court, and the strengths we bring to the game are football strengths. The art is to build on the strengths you have, not the ones you wish you had.

Look for the strengths you really have. When you look for the strengths you really have, you *find* the strengths you really have. Build on them. Expand one of them. You grow richer, fuller strengths along the way. If you look for the strengths you wish you had, you miss the strengths you already have. Claim your strengths. Expand one of your current strengths.

Add a New Strength

Now, do the third step. Add a new strength that builds on and matches with the strengths you have. God helps us add new strengths. Think through, pray about, and visit with wise, trusted mentors. Consider the one new strength to be like a new, close friend whom you would like to be part of your life.

Grow forward where you can grow forward.

Sometimes, in adding a new strength in our life, we think we should move to our weakest weaknesses, but once again we place ourselves in the weakest position to tackle our weaknesses. Oh, we might grow forward, but if we do, it is with difficulty and adversity. Do not head for your weakest weakness.

When you begin with your strengths, build on your strengths, and expand one of your strengths. Now, you are in the strongest position to add a new strength. In adding a new strength, look at some of your midrange strengths.

Some of the twelve keys for a healthy life you have well in place. They are lead strengths. On a scale of 1 to 10, 10 being high, they are 8, 9, or 10. Some are midrange. You have them in place as a 5, 6, or 7. They are not full strengths. They are on the way.

They can, with focus, be developed as new, full strengths. When you set out to add a new strength, look first at your midrange strengths. Develop one of these to full strength. If you want to do something with a weakness, then first select a midrange strength and add it. Then, having done so, you might select a weakness. The key, then, is to focus on a midrange strength first and only then a weakest weakness. You grow forward more easily than if you choose a weakest weakness to add as new strength.

The key is: add one new strength you can add, not ones you think you should or—what would be worse—one someone else thinks you should add. The art is to grow forward where you can grow forward.

You will notice that I encourage you to expand one current strength and to add one new strength. Sometimes, in our enthusiasm, we get carried away, trying to do too much too soon, and we find ourselves in a predicament.

One year, with much enthusiasm, three good friends, Gene, Charles, and yours truly, decided we would take 35mm slide pictures of all the work of our congregation across the course of the coming year. Thereby, during the stewardship campaign the following October, we would have the best three-screen, three-slide-projector, multimedia-with-background-music presentation of the mission of our congregation there had ever been.

With much enthusiasm, three cameras went busily click, click, click for a year. That fall, before the stewardship campaign, we gathered at the corner drugstore with all our little metal containers of film to have them developed. The druggist was delighted to see us. He could see early retirement. The condominium in Florida was finally at hand. When the druggist told us how much it was going to cost to develop all those little metal containers of film, our enthusiasm nose-dived.

We knew we were not that good at tunneling. It would take a tunnel to Fort Knox to acquire some of the gold to pay for developing all those little metal containers of film. In our enthusiasm we had failed to mark which little metal containers had which pictures. It had been for us an all-or-nothing project.

Forlorn, dejected, we headed for the door to puzzle out our next move. As we were nearing the door, the druggist hollered out, "Wait. I almost forgot. Eastman Kodak has just come out with self-developing kits. For a fraction of the cost, in the privacy of your own homes, you can develop the film yourselves."

Gene, Charles, and Ken have been known to be intrigued by new ventures and new projects, with much enthusiasm. This sounded even more interesting than we had originally thought. With our enthusiasm soaring, each of us bought a chemical kit and a developing tank.

Loaded down with our bundles and packages, we headed to the door. We were bubbling over with enthusiasm. As we were again almost at the door, the druggist hollered out, "Wait. I almost forgot to tell you. You must get the film from the little metal container into the developing tank without exposing it to a single ray of light. Once you get the film on the spool, put the spool into the tank, put the lid securely on the tank, then you can take the developing tank to the kitchen, with the lights on, pour the chemicals, and develop the film. This is so new a product I don't know quite how to tell you how to do it."

Still with renewed enthusiasm, confident we could figure something out, we headed to the door. We thought one or all of us could puzzle it through.

A couple of days later, my lifelong good friend, Gene, called saying, "Ken, come over tonight. I've figured it out." Charles and Ken gathered that evening, with much enthusiasm, at Gene's home.

We headed down the hall to Gene's bedroom, into Gene's bedroom closet. Three grown men, one little metal container of film, one developing tank. We closed the door.

We remembered what the druggist had told us. There was some light coming in at the top corner of the door. We opened the closet door and put Gene's bathrobe across the corner, closed the door, and blocked that light out.

There was some light coming in at the foot of the door. We took some of Gene's shoes and slippers and shoved them against the foot of the door, and blocked that light out.

There was still some light coming in around the keyhole and the door-knob. I took one of Gene's shirts and held it up against the keyhole and the doorknob to block out the last remaining ray of light.

So, now we could *watch* Gene *show* us how to take the film from the little metal container and place it into the developing tank *in absolute pitch darkness*.

Enthusiasm minus Planning equals a Dark Closet.

Well, we are in there. We decide Gene might as well get that one roll of film into the developing tank. He can then at least show us how to mix the chemicals. He gets the film out of the little metal container. Then—it is crowded with three of us in the closet—someone moves, causing him to drop the film. Now three grown men are searching for a stray sliver of film amid the shoes and slippers in pitch darkness.

Gene's good wife, Ann, comes to the door and knocks gently. "Everything all right in there? You've been in there an awfully long time."

There are more academic degrees gathered in that closet than you can imagine. Gene brings two degrees, including a master's in engineering. Charles brings three degrees. Yours truly brings four degrees, including a Ph.D., to the closet. I discover a pair of important learnings:

> Enthusiasm minus Planning equals a Dark Closet.
>
> Enthusiasm plus Planning equals a Solid Future.

Yes, we did develop the film. Yes, we did have the best three-screen, three-projector, multimedia-with-background-music presentation of the work and mission of our congregation. And yes, Ann, Gene's good wife, shared with Julie what had happened that night, and the word went out across the congregation. For several weeks, people would walk up to us, and just before they said hello they would almost burst out laughing. They could still see those three grown men in that dark closet.

I learned a helpful lesson that night. Sometimes, we allow our enthusiasm to carry us away. We try to do too much. We set ourselves up to fail. Enthusiasm is important. Planning is important. The two are good friends. They walk hand-in-hand toward a strong future.

The art of a whole, healthy life is to expand one of your present strengths and add one new strength. Yes, we are headed, in due course, to having nine of the twelve keys well in place. For now, we focus on a few. In our enthusiasm, we might try to do too much too soon and end up in a dark closet. Among the twelve keys, expand one and add one. Save some of the twelve keys for the future. For now, expand one and add one.

Selecting the Strengths to Expand and Add

Select the keys to grow that you would have fun growing. Consider the strengths that bring you a sense of good fun, good times. The ones you have fun doing are God's way of teaching you the ones to focus on. Not that it is easy. There may be difficulty. You bring your fullest resources to expanding and adding these strengths. You concentrate some of your deepest energy, intellect, emotions, will, and prayer to growing these strengths. With all of that, select the strengths you would have fun developing.

Focus on the strengths that have value beyond yourself. Consider the strengths that have value with your family and friends, that advance the quality of your life together. It is not that you should grow those that would please your family and friends. Rather, think through the strengths you can develop that contribute to a healthier family environment, fuller and deeper relationships, a constructive, growing future with your family and friends. Consider the strengths that have promise for a constructive future for your community and world. Grow these strengths first.

Select the keys you can grow forward in a simple way. The simpler your approach, the more likely you are to succeed. A complex approach, precisely because it is complex, stirs a pattern of exhilaration and depression. Excess breeds excess. There is exhilaration and excitement, at the beginning, like the rise to the top of the roller coaster, because we are launching a complex, grandiose venture "to improve ourselves." The exhilaration is followed quickly by rushing depression, to the bottom. This is followed by a new high, a new low, and new curves and twists, until we are exhausted. It may be fun to ride an amusement park roller coaster from time to time. It is not the way to advance one's life.

The promise of the Gospel is in Jesus' words, "I am come that they might have life, and that they might have it more abundantly" (John 10:10 KJV). God wants for you a strong, healthy life. This is not some Pollyanna, naïve, whistling-in-the-dark, foolish optimism. Life brings problems and weaknesses. They are real, present, a source of troublement and concern. But if we become preoccupied with our problems, we end up neglecting our strengths. Strengths are like muscles. Well used, strengths grow and develop. Sometimes we overlook, neglect, or ignore our strengths. Not used, they atrophy. If we disregard our strengths, they decline. They wither.

Begin with your strengths. Claim God's gifts. Build on your strengths. Select one strength to expand and one strength to add. You will develop the abundant life Christ gives you. When we are down on ourselves, distracted by our problems, in an almost self-destructive mode, we disparage, scorn, and repudiate our strengths. Sometimes we misuse, abuse, and mistreat our strengths. This quiet rage is not helpful to us and does not advance our best strengths. We are instead invited to a biblically based, God-centered understanding of life. We are invited to grow forward our strengths, God's gifts.

One Time

Discover the one strength you plan to expand and the one you plan to add. Grow each forward in one-time actions. Give it a go. One time. Try it. One time. There are several ways people grow forward:

- A one-time action
- A seasonal effort, usually periodically from one year to the next
- A short-term effort, usually three to five times over several weeks or months
- A long-term effort, usually six-plus times over several weeks or months
- A weekly, monthly, year-round effort over a long period of time

Focus on a one-time action. For an excellent sprinter, a one-time action works. For a solid marathon runner, a one-time action works too. Do something one time. See if it helps. If it does, do it another time. Then, another time. Expand its value in a sequence of one-time actions.

If you do a "one time" and it helps you grow, do another "one time." Do not immediately turn the one time into a weekly, monthly, year-round plan. Do another one-time action. You may go for several weeks or months doing essentially the same thing on a one-time basis.

Some people have learned to be excellent sprinters. They do what they do in short, highly intensive ways near the time at hand. Some people have learned to be solid marathon runners. They do what they do steadfastly, regularly, routinely, weekly and monthly, year-round. Your competencies for growing yourself may be as an excellent sprinter, or as a solid marathon runner. God blesses both.

Regrettably, too many books written on personal growth and self-improvement are written by solid marathon runners. Sometimes, it takes a solid marathon runner to write the book. There are a great many marathon runners who write books. Thus, the counsel on personal growth is frequently hammered out that the only way to grow is to be committed to a long-term, arduous, routine, weekly, monthly, year-round schedule for self-improvement.

The truth is people grow in lots of one-time, seasonal, short-term ways, as well as long-term, weekly, monthly, year-round ways. Focus first on one-time actions to grow a given strength. Then, as the strength grows, you can explore some of the other ways and see what helps you. How you go about your growth contributes to your growth. It is both what you do and how you go about it. Do something for your growth one time. Then, try a seasonal way, maybe once a year. On occasion, you might try a short-term project approach, three to five sessions for your growth. Now and then, consider a long-term project, six-plus sessions, to assist your growth. Consider, perhaps at some point, a weekly or monthly, year-round way. Begin your growth with one-time actions that help you grow you.

Keep It Straightforward

We know it helps to keep it straightforward. We are looking for one or two specific objectives to expand a current strength. In our enthusiasm, and perhaps in our compulsiveness toward perfectionism, we come up with five to ten specific objectives. What takes wisdom is selecting the one or two objectives that help you in the simplest fashion.

For example, one of your current strengths among the twelve keys may be compassion. On a scale of 1 to 10, you have this strength well in place as an 8. You decide this is a strength you want to expand in your life. Look at the specific components of compassion:

○ I have steady, quiet humility.

○ I enjoy sharing and being with people.

○ I have a deep love for people.

○ I receive and share forgiveness generously and fully.

You discover you have the first three components well in place. You decide the one component you want to grow is your capacity to receive and share forgiveness. That is your specific objective. Now, do a one-time. One time, for some specific event in your life, receive God's forgiveness. One time, with some one person who has damaged and harmed you, share your forgiveness.

It is not that you grow your capacity for forgiveness by trying to receive God's forgiveness for everything, or that you try somehow mustering up all your courage and will, to forgive each and every person who has damaged and harmed you. Receive God's forgiveness one time for one event. Share your forgiveness one time with one person. You are on your way. Do another one-time. Another one-time. Practice forgiveness in one-time actions. Compassion grows.

Perhaps one of the new strengths among the twelve keys you want to add is encouragement. On a scale of 1 to 10, you have this strength in place in the midrange, as a 5. You decide this is a strength you want to add in your life. Look at the specific components of encouragement:

○ I share the gift of "well done" with persons around me.

○ I live a life of grace.

○ I have a sense of humor.

○ I live a life of progress.

You discover you have the second and third components well in place. You decide the two you want to grow are the first and fourth, your capacity to share the gift of "well done" and to live a life of progress. These are your two specific objectives. Frankly, if you grow either one of the two forward, the strength of encouragement grows in you. If you grow, for example, your ability to live a life of progress, with that one component your whole life advances. You can decide to focus on only one of the two, or you can decide to focus on one this year and the other in the year to come.

To learn "well done," do a one-time. Receive God's "well done" one time for one thing you have done well. Receive God's "well done" for a second thing you have done well. Share "well done" with one person one time. It is not that you grow your capacity for sharing "well done" by trying to say "well done" for everything. Share "well done" one time with one person. You are on your way. Do another one-time. Another one-time. Practice "well done" in one-time acts. Encouragement grows.

To learn a life of progress, do a one-time. Pick one day. Live for this one day a life of progress, not perfectionism. Be at peace this one day. Experience serenity this one day. You are on your way. Do another one-time. Another one-time. Practice progress in one-time ways. A life of progress is developed through a progression of one-time acts.

Indeed, any determination to live a life of progress from now on fails because that "from now on" is a compulsion to perfectionism. We are done in before we have begun. *How* we grow ourselves is as important as the direction we grow.

Be at peace. Do not even become compulsive about living progress on a one-day basis. A compulsion to progress gets close to an addiction to perfectionism; both are addictions. Simply, live progress this one day, simply, one day at a time. Encouragement will grow. Your whole life will grow forward.

For many of us, if we learn to live a life of progress, one day at a time, this one learning can shape our whole life. This one learning is worth the whole of life's journey. This one learning enriches our lives and the lives of those around us. This one learning has spillover value in the whole of our lives.

So you see, it is not so much that you become busy about your growth. It is more like this. Pick one strength among the twelve keys you want to expand. Look at the four components of that strength. Find the one of the four that is the one way, for you, to expand that strength. Do that one way one time. Do another one, one time. As we act, so we become.

Pick one strength among the twelve keys you want to add. Look at the four components of that strength. Find the one of the four that is the one way, for you, to add that strength. Do that one way one time. Do another one, one time. God blesses your growth.

God invites us to live a life of grace, not law. Approach your growth with a spirit of grace, not law. You do not need a long list of ninety-seven resolutions and mandates that you must carry out, weekly, monthly, year-round, in order to grow a given strength in your life. Someone who shows you a list like that is inviting you to law, not grace.

Live what works for you. Grow yourself in the ways that help you. Use your creativity and flexibility. Experiment. Explore. There is no one right way for all persons to grow. In fact, there are multiple ways you can grow yourself. Discover the ones that work well for you now.

Do not start drawing up long lists of the things you have to do for each of the twelve keys for a healthy life. Such lists start out as possibilities. But they quickly become probabilities. Then, probabilities become axioms. Axioms quickly become law. Law quickly becomes a long list of shoulds, oughts, musts, do's and don'ts. The spirit of what we are about is grace. Stay with grace. You will do well.

Sometimes we are much like the group who gathered in the early years of AA. We get carried away, busily writing down a long list of rules. We create a series of rules and regulations, conditions and stipulations, policies and procedures, all law. Don't take yourself too seriously. We are invited to not get too attached to the complex, tidy plans for growth we keep trying to impose on ourselves. We are invited to not become addictive about our growth and development.

AA is built on a one-time approach to one's growth. The focus is one day at a time. The encouragement is to work one's growth plan at whatever pace helps. The focus is to not get too addicted to one's growth. The focus is that we all grow in our own pilgrimage in whatever ways help us.

Life is like a fast break down the basketball court, like a jazz improvisational group, like a drama repertoire company, like an "audible" called at the line of scrimmage. Life is not a complex, tidy game plan where we slowly, methodically bring the ball down the court, or where we know exactly each note we plan to play, or we stick only to lines in a rigid script, or only call the plays planned before the start of the game.

We live one day at a time. We are flexible. We look for new insights. We find what works for us. We discover new ways. From one month to the next, from one year to the next, from one life stage to the next, we focus on growing certain of the twelve keys for a healthy life, expanding this one, adding that one. As time moves on, we can expand yet another one, add yet new ones.

We know this. It does not take a long list of resolutions, a lengthy tabulation of good intentions, a protracted register of rules. In our eagerness we may make the mistake of trying to do too much, too soon, too impatiently. Growing ourselves takes a few objectives that are specific and concrete, realistic and achievable, with solid time horizons. God invites us to grow forward in ways we can.

Act

Act on your future. God is with you. God wants for you a richer, fuller life. God leads you forward. Stir. Move. Grow. Do it today. Create a simple action plan that helps you grow you. Act. Now.

$$P \rightarrow B \rightarrow D$$

Perception yields behavior. Behavior yields destiny. Live now the future you seek. That future will be yours. Behave the way you want to be. You will become how you behave.

Do not allow those old, old ghosts—compulsiveness toward perfectionism; postponing procrastination; a pervasive sense of powerlessness; "analysis paralysis"; wishful thinking; excessive drive toward achievement; the memory of past failures, disappointments, and tragedies; the sorrow of past guilts and griefs—do not allow these frail old shadows to haunt you or dissuade you. Act now.

Growing a healthy life is not so much a matter of longer hours, determination and drive, hard work and tenacity. We sometimes imagine the more committed we are and the harder we work, the better our life will be. When we work harder, we get more tired. Things don't automatically get better. When we work harder, headed in the wrong direction, toward our weaknesses, we just get there quicker and faster.

Act now the way you want life to be. You will become the future you live out now. As one ancient text has it,

> Sow a thought, reap an action,
> Sow an action, reap a habit,
> Sow a habit, reap a character,
> Sow a character, reap a destiny.

As you think, so you act. As you act, so you become. The full way forward, the art of developing a strong, healthy life is in these four steps:

1. I claim my strengths.
2. I expand a current strength.
3. I add a new strength.
4. I act on my future today.

You will live a whole, healthy life. Pray these words. Put these words where you see them each day. Say these words. Live these words. Your life will be full, whole, rich, and healthy.

The Kingdom of God

Jesus describes the kingdom of God as a great banquet. Jesus does not describe the kingdom of God as dull and boring, glum and gloomy, dreary and dismal. We have bleak, monotonous, tedious, torpid times in life. When you think of the life God wants for you, think of the wonder and joy, the laughter, the good fun at a great banquet.

Jesus describes the kingdom of God as a wedding feast. Life sometimes brings dark, tragic times. We walk in the valley of the shadow. And when we live in the kingdom, we live in the hope and new life, the happiness and merriment, the good fun, the good times of a wedding feast.

God invites us to live in the kingdom, in this life, to experience the wonder and joy of God's love for us, to share in the compassion and community of the kingdom, to live in confidence and assurance, to live in the hope of the Holy Spirit in our lives.

This life is a great banquet of God's grace. This life is a wedding feast of God's hope. In the spirit of God's grace and hope, select the new strengths you plan to develop—with a sense of wonder and joy, laughter and good fun. Grow the strengths that bring a new happiness, a good spirit, good times to your life.

———— o ————

We are the people of mission and service.
We are the people of love and compassion.
We are the people of hope and new life, prayer and worship.
We are the people of community, roots, place, belonging.
We are the people of leadership and power.
We are the people of the simple life.
We are the people of joy and wonder.
We are the people of wisdom and judgment, vision and common sense.
We are the people of encouragement and confidence.
We are the people of creativity and future.
We are the people of health and vitality.
We are the people of generosity and giving. Amen.

16

THE FUTURE FOR YOU

LIFE IS A SEARCH. Life is a pilgrimage. We make our fair share of mistakes. Sometimes more than we wish. Sometimes we learn from our mistakes. Sometimes we learn just enough from our mistakes that we can move on.

Life is peace and panic, fear and release, qualms and quiet, fear and anxiety, calmness and conflict, forgiving and reconciling, tears and compassion, worry and calm, tragedy and wonder, sorrow and cheer, old ways and new discoveries, doubt and death, hope and new ways. Life gives us a range of experiences: honest and horrific, humorous and holy.

Life is laughter and sadness, joy and despair, good times and dark tragedy, faith and fright, a mingling of confidence and assurance, doubt and dread, security and fright, serenity and bravery. Life is birthday parties and toothaches, birds singing and dark storms. Life is happiness and gladness, awe and humility, jealousy and generosity.

There are moments of accomplishment and achievement. There are flashes of dusky rage and raw terror. There are times of passive-aggressive behavior, low-grade hostility, subliminal resentment, and eruptive anger. There are events of wonder and joy, new life and hope. There are times when we feel the lowest of the lowest, and there are times we mount like eagles to the heavens.

Life is simple, and life is complex. It is now one thing, and then it is another. There are good surprises, cheerful moments, deep passion, great love. There are moments when we are brimming over with joy. There are times of confusion and retreat.

Life has its quiet times, peaceful and tranquil, and its noisy times. There are harsh, hard times, and pleasant, delightful times. We are awkward and anxious. We are upset and afraid. We discover excellent ideas and good suggestions. We have questions and puzzlements. There are moments of promise and faith. There are confident times.

We move forward and slide backward. Progress is our friend. Defeat overtakes us. Power and hope join us. Defeat and tragedy do us in. Sorrow and grief abide with us. Faith and hope and love lead us.

We are children. We are adults. We are something in between. We act graciously, and thoughtlessly. We act with consideration, and with haste. We gossip too much, and we are politely silent.

We are careless and neglectful, foolish and irrational. Impulsive and awkward. Generous and giving. Scared and scarred. Selfish and stingy. Timid and cautious. Brave and bold. We live in fear. We do courageous deeds.

Death haunts us, and resurrection is our hope.

We long for the habits that encourage us to be highly helpful people. But life is not as simple as seven habits for highly effective people. Sometimes we are effective. Sometimes we are not. We do want our life to count, to be helpful.

God invites us to a life of service, not a life of survival. God encourages us to the enduring sacrament of compassion, not the frail altar of worldly success.

Life is a search. We are drawn to movements that help us fulfill, for this time, our deepest yearnings and longings, our foundational life searches.

In the end, success is service. The fleetly flimsies of this life come and go, wither and vanish. What remains, what endures are acts of kindness, moments of compassion, events of community, the sharing of service.

You Are Your Future

What you do with you shapes your future. Emerging trends rise and fall. Some things come and go. Good surprises come your way. Tragic events darken your life. Sinful events weigh you down. Take their toll. Anxiety and anger visit you. Doubt and disbelief come to you.

Good fun and good times bless your life. Wonder and joy are your friends. Progress leads you. Hope comforts you. Grace and love surround you. Amidst all of these happenings, how you relate to these events shapes your future. We are living on the threshold of a new age of hope in the history of humankind. It is what you do with this new time that gives you your future.

It is how you grow you that is decisive. You can control you. You cannot control the events and people around you. You can control how you relate to the events and persons in your life. Events swirl swiftly and suddenly. People do this, and then they do that. They are less than predictable. Amidst the changes that abound, you can control you. Have this confidence and assurance.

Grace is stronger than law.
  We are the people of grace.
Compassion is stronger than legalism.
  We are the people of compassion.
Easter is stronger than Good Friday.
  We are the Easter people.
The open tomb is stronger than the bloodied cross.
  We are the people of the open tomb.
The Risen Lord is stronger than the dead Jesus.
  We are the people of the Risen Lord.
    We are the resurrection people.
    We are the people of hope.

Know the grace of God, the love of Christ, the power and comfort of the Holy Spirit. Gather your mentors around you. Choose a sponsor who is a good resource for you. Do lots of one-time events to grow yourself. You are your future.

You Are the Future

One person. A small group. A large group. A whole movement. Each of these has been known to change the course of the future. It is not simply that the future unfolds before us and we try to do the best we can with what develops.

Callahan's Principle of the Future is this:

The future will be different than most projections of it suggest.

The other way I express the principle is this: the future will turn out differently than the experts predict. To be sure, a few projections may come to pass, but finally the only certainty is there is no certainty. Nothing lasts forever. Most predictions of the future do not come to pass. Most forecasts of the future do not happen.

What does happen is that the future comes into being because one person, a small group, a large group, a whole movement decides on a future, they head toward that future, and that way forward becomes the future.

The future does not come about because of trends and analyses, projections and prognostications. Oh, to the extent that people believe such things, roll over, and play dead, and behave and act as though they might happen, to that extent people allow such projections to become self-fulfilling prophecies.

Mostly, some person or group decides on a course of action and the future happens.

I say this not so that you become excessively engaged in changing the future. Most people who try to change the future miss my point. It is not so much that one person or a group is *trying* to change the future. It is more as if they have a course of action, a mission, an idea, a sense of direction. Their passion, their compassion, their commitment is to their course of action, not to changing the future. In the process of living out their course of action, the future is changed.

Count on this. The future will be different than most projections of it suggest. Some one person or group will come along, have a passion for where they are headed, and in the process the future is changed.

They Did

Peter was standing on the shore. He didn't know what to do next. He said, "Well, I guess I'll go back to fishing."

Some of the disciples were with him. They did not know what to do next either. They said, "Well, I guess we'll go with you."

Old ways die hard.

There had been three rich, full years with Christ. The teachings, the miracles, the crowds, the times away, the wonders. There had been Palm Sunday, Gethsemane, Golgotha, hiding, upper room, death. There had been open tomb, resurrection, risen Lord.

With all the wonder and joy, all the new hope and new life of those amazing three years and their experiences with their risen Lord, they did not now know what to do next. So they went back to the old ways.

They went out fishing all night. They tried all their favorite fishing places: over there, and over there, over there, almost desperately they tried yet over there. They used to catch fish in all these places, but they were turning up nothing.

I want you to sense the despair, depression, despondency that began to fill their boat about three o'clock that morning. You see, none of the places where they used to catch fish worked. They were good fishermen, and they were catching nothing.

Not even the old ways worked anymore.

Early that morning, sunrise coming, they were headed to shore. A stranger was standing on the shore. The setting is very clear. It is Jesus, and they do not know that it is Jesus. The stranger hollers out, "Have you caught any good fish?"

Now, what would any good fisherman known for making a living at catching fish—yea, even a recreational fisherman—usually say? "Yes." The fish get even bigger and bigger each time we tell our tales.

But this time, there is an almost plaintive plea—you can almost hear the despair in the answer: "No, we haven't caught any fish."

The stranger says, "Cast your nets on the starboard side of the boat."

Someone might suggest that the point is that we have been living too long with older patterns of behavior and that Christ now invites us to grow forward in fresh, new ways. Some one might suggest that. Surely not yours truly. That is not the point.

The point of the text, the miracle in the story, is in the words, "They did."

We sometimes think the miracle is that the nets are now so loaded with fish that the fishermen can hardly bring them into the boat. That is the second miracle. The first miracle is "They did."

You see, this is a stranger. All they know is that a stranger has invited them to cast their nets on the other side of the boat. The miracle is "They did."

They could row the other way. They could have a committee meeting. They could have a long, lengthy discussion. They could develop a ninety-seven page, long-range plan for fishing for the coming ten years.

The miracle is, even when Christ comes to us as a stranger, we discover new ways in Christ.

Yes, old ways die hard. We do discover new ways in Christ. We grow and learn. We develop and build. The second miracle is that the nets are loaded with fish.

The third miracle is in the words, "It is the Lord." What I learn from those words is this: cast your nets, you will see Christ. It is not that we discover Christ and then go and do the mission. It is in the sharing of the mission that we discover Christ. It is in serving people with compassion and hope that we find God.

Remember what the angel says to the women: "And tell the disciples that Christ has gone before them into Galilee." Christ has gone before them into the mission. It is not that first we grow ourselves forward and *then* we go share in the mission. It is in the sharing of the mission that we grow forward. It is in serving people with their human hurts and hopes that we discover Christ.

Where is Christ? Christ lives and dies and is risen again and again among the human hurts and hopes of the people God has planted all around us. That is where Christ is. That is where God is.

There is a fourth miracle. As the boat gets to shore, Jesus says to them, "Come and have breakfast." I learn this from the text: Christ cares for your every need.

Christ understands the disciples have been fishing all night long. The old ways have not worked. They are tired and hungry. There is no long lecture. There is no list of commandments. There is no "Why haven't you figured it out in the past three years?"

There is simply, "Come and have breakfast."

Count on—depend upon—this. God cares for your every need. May God's blessings of growing and developing, grace and peace, hope and new life be ever with you and yours. God bless you. God be with you. Come. Your new life is ready.

A BLESSING FOR YOUR LIFE

May the mission of God lead you.
   May the compassion of God surround you.
     May the hope of God go before you.
May the community of God bless you.
   May the leading of God grow you.
     May the simplicity of God give you peace.
May the joy of God strengthen you.
   May the wisdom of God guide you.
     May the encouragement of God lift you.
May the creativity of God stir you.
   May the health of God heal you.
     May the generosity of God give you grace. Amen.

A GUIDE FOR EXPLORING YOUR LIFE POSSIBILITIES

YOU WILL FIND THIS GUIDE to your life possibilities helpful. You are welcome to use it to consider where your current strengths are, and to decide the strengths you look forward to advancing in your own life.

The guide is suggestive, flexible. It provides clues to where you are and where you can be. It encourages possibilities for your growth. It is not intended as law: rigid, unyielding. Do not turn it into rules and regulations, requirements and restrictions, legalisms and ordinances. It is a clue for your growth. It gives hints and signs of how you can grow yourself in your daily life.

Where You Are Now

1. With your best wisdom, consider where you are for the four resources in each key, ranging from 1 to 25 points, with 25 the highest rating. For each key, the matching chapter helps you discover your personal rating.

2. Enter your rating numbers in the blanks and add together the four scores to discover the total for each of the twelve keys. Divide the total for each guide by 10 to discover your current growth on a scale of 1 to 10.

3. Circle where you are on the Twelve Keys for Living Chart on p. 184.

Here's an example:

	Maximum score	Your points	Rating
COMPASSION			
I have steady, quiet humility.	25	20	
I enjoy sharing and being with people.	25	25	
I have a deep love for people.	25	25	
I receive and share forgiveness generously and fully.	25	10	
Total		80	8

80 divided by 10 equals 8. Circle 8 on the Twelve Keys Chart for this item.

COMPASSION

1 2 3 4 5 6 7 ⑧ 9 10

Moving Forward

Once you have circled all of your ratings on the Twelve Keys for Living Chart on p. 184, follow these steps:

1. Claim your current strengths: underline your 8s, 9s, and 10s.
2. Expand one current strength: underline a second time one strength that you plan to develop further.
3. Add one new strength: circle one strength, a 1 to a 7, that you plan to grow to an 8.
4. Act on your plan: decide on your one-time actions.

LIFE POSSIBILITIES GUIDES

	Maximum score	Your points	Rating
MISSION			
My mission, my purpose in life lives out my longings.	25	____	
My mission, my purpose matches my competencies.	25	____	
The help I share is freely given.	25	____	
I share concrete, effective help.	25	____	
Total		____	____
COMPASSION			
I have steady, quiet humility.	25	____	
I enjoy sharing and being with people.	25	____	
I have a deep love for people.	25	____	
I receive and share forgiveness generously and fully.	25	____	
Total		____	____
HOPE			
I value and learn from memory.	25	____	
I see hope in the present and immediate future.	25	____	
I see sources of hope in the distant future.	25	____	
I have confidence there is hope in the next life.	25	____	
Total		____	____
COMMUNITY			
I have a sense of roots in my life.	25	____	
I have a sense of place.	25	____	
I experience a sense of belonging.	25	____	
I have a sense of family and friends.	25	____	
Total		____	____

	Maximum score	Your points	Rating
LEADERSHIP			
I am proactive and intentional about how I lead my life.	25	____	
I share a sense of balance with people around me.	25	____	
I am rediscovering a sense of power in my life.	25	____	
I have the capacity to deal with conflict.	25	____	
Total		____	____
SIMPLICITY			
I have a healthy approach in making decisions.	25	____	
I have the ability to deal with change.	25	____	
I have a balanced capacity in gathering things.	25	____	
I work well with others.	25	____	
Total		____	____
JOY			
I have a sense of wonder about life.	25	____	
I have learned to relax and have fun.	25	____	
I have the ability to express my feelings.	25	____	
I live in and trust God.	25	____	
Total		____	____
WISDOM			
I have a sense of meekness before the truth.	25	____	
I have the benefit of helpful mentors in my life.	25	____	
I have a sense of vision for my life.	25	____	
I have common sense in living life.	25	____	
Total		____	____

	Maximum score	Your points	Rating

ENCOURAGEMENT

I share the gift of "well done" with people.	25	____	
I live a life of grace.	25	____	
I have a sense of humor.	25	____	
I live a life of progress.	25	____	
Total		____	____

CREATIVITY

I learn from my mistakes.	25	____	
I learn from my achievements.	25	____	
I have a spirit of flexibility.	25	____	
I learn in a rich variety of ways.	25	____	
Total		____	____

HEALTH

I appreciate and value the gift of life.	25	____	
I have some capacity to deal with the presence of death.	25	____	
I have a positive attitude about my health.	25	____	
I feed my spirit in mission and prayer.	25	____	
Total		____	____

GENEROSITY

I live a life of modest financial needs.	25	____	
I value myself in more ways than money.	25	____	
I develop the financial resources with which I am blessed.	25	____	
I share my blessings and giving with many persons and causes.	25	____	
Total		____	____

TWELVE KEYS FOR LIVING
Possibilities for a
Whole, Healthy Life

MISSION
1 2 3 4 5 6 7 8 9 10

COMPASSION
1 2 3 4 5 6 7 8 9 10

HOPE
1 2 3 4 5 6 7 8 9 10

COMMUNITY
1 2 3 4 5 6 7 8 9 10

LEADERSHIP
1 2 3 4 5 6 7 8 9 10

SIMPLICITY
1 2 3 4 5 6 7 8 9 10

JOY
1 2 3 4 5 6 7 8 9 10

WISDOM
1 2 3 4 5 6 7 8 9 10

ENCOURAGEMENT
1 2 3 4 5 6 7 8 9 10

CREATIVITY
1 2 3 4 5 6 7 8 9 10

HEALTH
1 2 3 4 5 6 7 8 9 10

GENEROSITY
1 2 3 4 5 6 7 8 9 10

Claim your current strengths: underline your 8s, 9s, 10s

Expand one current strength: underline a second time one strength to develop further

Add one new strength: circle one strength, a 1 to 7, to grow to an 8

Act on your plan: decide on your one-time actions

Growing Your Life Forward

Well done. You now have a simple, effective plan to grow forward a whole, healthy life. You are building on your strengths, to do better what you do best.

Set the date to advance your plan. It could be one month, three months, or six months from now.

As you advance your plan, accomplish three things:

1. Celebrate new learnings.

   Look back on the growth objectives you set for yourself.

   Celebrate those you have achieved.

   Consider what you have learned in achieving these objectives.

   Share prayers of thanks and celebration for what you have accomplished, what you have learned, how you have grown.

2. Continue to advance your plan.

   Look ahead to your future growth. Improve your plan. You may want to delete or revise some objectives. You may want to include some new objectives.

3. Add your new time frame

   You may be looking three months ahead. At the end of the first month, you advance your plan (step 2). You improve what you hope to achieve in the second and third months of your growth. Now, add the new third month.

This is a dynamic approach to your growth.

Your sense of action, satisfaction, growth, and development will be greatly strengthened.

You will be helpful in the lives and destinies of many persons.

God bless you. God be with you.

THE AUTHOR

DR. KENNON L. CALLAHAN—researcher, professor, and pastor—is one of today's most sought-after church consultants. He has worked with thousands of congregations around the world and has helped tens of thousands of church leaders and pastors through his dynamic workshops and seminars. Author of ten books, he is best known for his groundbreaking study *Twelve Keys to an Effective Church*, which formed the basis for the Mission Growth Movement, a widely acclaimed program for church renewal. Callahan has earned the B.A., M.Div., S.T.M., and Ph.D. degrees. His Ph.D. is in Systematic Theology. He has served both rural and urban congregations in Ohio, Texas, and Georgia and taught for many years at Emory University.

Ken and Julie, his wife of over forty years, have two children, Ken and Mike, and three grandchildren, Blake, Mason, and Brice. They enjoy the outdoors, hiking, horseback riding, and camping.

INDEX

A

Achievement, excessive drive toward, 121

Achievements, capacity to learn from, 128–129

Acquisition, 87–88

Act, 170–171

Advice, versus encouragement, 117

Aelyppius, 100

Al-Anon, 77

Alcoholics Anonymous, 77, 105, 118, 169

Anchor story, 34

Anger, 76, 98

Anthropology, 58

Anxiety, 85

Apathy, 76

Appalachia, 49

Archeology, 58

Aristotle, 103

Augustine, 101

Australia, 131

B

Bahamas, 34, 126

Balance, sense of, 73–75

Basketball story, 159–161

Behavior, 170

Belonging, sense of: four levels of, 64; and groups, 62–63; and identity, 63; and sense of continuity and consistency, 63

Benefaction, and striking gift, 14

Bimini, 125

Bobby, 1–5

Brady Lake Elementary School, 17

C

Callahan, J. M., 30

Callahan principle of the future, 175

Callahan principle of wisdom, 110

Certainty, 47

Change, dealing with, 86–87

Chariots of Fire, 24

Christmas, 44

Cliff people, 50–51

Codependency, pattern of, 24, 25

Codependent-dependent pattern of relationships, 7–8

Common sense, and wisdom, 108–110

Communications, networks of, 61

Community: as key for living, 53–67; search for, 22; and sense of belonging, 62–64; and sense of family and friends, 64–67; and sense of place, 59–62; and sense of roots, 56

Compassion: and deep love for people, 33; and forgiving, 33–36; and grace, 37; and humility, 30–32; as key for living, 29–38; and sharing, 32

Competencies: matching of, to serving, 20; sharing of, 22

Confession, 126

Confidence, 118

Conflict, capacity to deal with, 77–80

Consequentiality, 109

Constantine, 101

Q

Quilting group story, 29–30

R

Reciprocity, mutual, 61
Regional, versus local, in sense of place, 60–62
Resentment, 36, 37
River people, 50
Roman Empire, 100–101
Roots, sense of, 56–58
Rule 63 (Alcoholics Anonymous), 118, 119
Ruskin, J., 80

S

Sacrifice, 25
Sam, 113–114
Self-destruction, 7
Self-esteem, 21, 31, 104, 144
Self-fulfilling prophecy, 9
Self-protective measures, 25
Self-reliance, spirit of, 24
Sense of humor, 118–119
Serenity, 123
Serving, versus surviving, 18
"Shall We Gather at the River," 49
Sharing: and blessings, 153–154; and compassion, 32; and competencies, 22; and feelings, 99; and gift of "well done," 114–116; and grace, 22–24; and joy, 99; and service, 21
Simplicity: and dealing with change, 86–87; and gathering things, 87–88; as key to life, 83–90; and making decisions, 84–86; and working together, 89–90
Societal dislocation, 57, 66
Softball story (Bobby), 1–5
Specific objectives, 96
Spillover impact, 13–14

Spirit, feeding the, 145–146
Star Trek, 109
Star Wars, 27
Status, 26
Straightforwardness, 167–170
Strengths, 45; and action, 170–171; and addition of new strength, 162–165; and claiming personal strengths, 5–6; and expansion of current strengths, 158–162; and Kingdom of God, 170–171; and one-time actions, 166–167; selection of, for expansion and addition, 165–167; and specific objectives, 167–170
Success, preoccupation with, 21
Survival instincts, 18

T

Tegast, 100
Things, gathering of, 87–88
Tom, 147–148
Travel, networks of, 61
Tribbles, 109
Twelve keys for living: and community, 53–67; and compassion, 29–38; and creativity, 125–137; and encouragement, 113–123; and generosity, 147–154; and health, 139–146; and hope, 39–52; and joy, 93–102; and leadership, 69–80; and mission, 17–27; and simplicity, 83–90; and wisdom, 103–110
Twelve Keys for Living chart, 179, 180, 184
Twelve Step program, 106
Two-for-one principle, 129

V

Value, trust in, 151
Valuing: and gift of life, 139–141; and oneself, 150–151

Vision, 107–108; versus idealism, 108
Vocational village, 65

W

Washington, D.C., 75
Weaknesses: focus on, 6, 66, 128
Wisdom: and common sense,
108–110; as key for living,
103–110; meekness as beginning
of, 104–105; and mentors,
105–107; and vision, 107–108
Wonder: and possibilities for whole
happy life, 14; sense of, 95
Work group, 65
Working together, 89–90